BRIGHT NOTES

THE RIME OF THE ANCIENT MARINER AND OTHER WORKS BY SAMUEL TAYLOR COLERIDGE

Intelligent Education

Nashville, Tennessee

BRIGHT NOTES: The Rime of the Ancient Mariner and Other Works
www.BrightNotes.com

No part of this publication may be used or reproduced in any manner whatsoever without written permission, except in the case of brief quotations in critical articles and reviews. For permissions, contact Influence Publishers http://www.influencepublishers.com.

ISBN: 978-1-645423-86-7 (Paperback)
ISBN: 978-1-645423-87-4 (eBook)

Published in accordance with the U.S. Copyright Office Orphan Works and Mass Digitization report of the register of copyrights, June 2015.

Originally published by Monarch Press.
John W. Elliott, 1965
2020 Edition published by Influence Publishers.

Interior design by Lapiz Digital Services. Cover Design by Thinkpen Designs.

Printed in the United States of America.

Library of Congress Cataloging-in-Publication Data forthcoming.
Names: Intelligent Education
Title: BRIGHT NOTES: The Rime of the Ancient Mariner and Other Works
Subject: STU004000 STUDY AIDS / Book Notes

CONTENTS

1)	Introduction to Samuel Taylor Coleridge	1
2)	Introduction to The Rime of the Ancient Mariner	28
3)	Textual Analysis	36
	The Rime of the Ancient Mariner: Part I	36
	The Rime of the Ancient Mariner: Part II	42
	The Rime of the Ancient Mariner: Part III	48
	The Rime of the Ancient Mariner: Part IV	55
	The Rime of the Ancient Mariner: Part V	64
	The Rime of the Ancient Mariner: Part VI	75
	The Rime of the Ancient Mariner: Part VII	84
4)	The Rime of the Ancient Mariner: Essay Questions And Answers	94
5)	Introduction to Christabel	101
6)	Textual Analysis	106
	Christabel: Part I	106
	Christabel: Part II	124
7)	Christabel: Essay Questions And Answers	147

8)	Introduction to Kubla Khan	152
9)	Kubla Khan Interpretation: The Main Theme	168
10)	Kubla Khan: Essay Questions And Answers	180
11)	Introduction to Dejection: An Ode	184
12)	Dejection: An Ode: The Poem	191
13)	Dejection: An Ode: Essay Questions And Answers	213
14)	What Critics Have Said	217
15)	Bibliography	227

SAMUEL TAYLOR COLERIDGE

INTRODUCTION

....

| INTRODUCTION

With very few exceptions Coleridge's really good poetry - certainly all of his great poetry - was written by the time he was thirty. Since this book is a study of Coleridge's poetry, not of his prose (of which there is plenty), the biographical summary that follows does not extend, except as a sketch, beyond 1802. It does attempt some detail of analysis of his life and involvements through 1802, the years during which he was a poet and was becoming one. There is an effort made to review with considerable attention the deep friendship and enriching relationship that Coleridge for several years found with William and Dorothy Wordsworth.

Coleridge's letters are the best biographical source we have for the very good reason that he wrote so many. There was in his personality a very deep need to express himself to his friends and acquaintances on practically everything he thought or felt. Some passages from his letters are quoted here for the valuable insight they give into the man's mind, which speaks most times more eloquently than anyone could speak for it.

DATE AND PLACE OF BIRTH

Named for one of his godfathers, Samuel Taylor Coleridge was born in the late morning of 20 October, a Wednesday in the calendar of 1772. Coleridge's father was the son of John Coleridge of Crediton, both a weaver and woolen draper. Coleridge's mother, Anne Bowden, was of Devon origins. The name of the town in which Coleridge was born is Ottery St. Mary. At the time, his father, the Reverend John Coleridge, was Vicar of the Parish, Master of the King's New Grammar School, and Chaplain Priest of the Collegiate Church. Ottery remains much as it was in 1772.

COLERIDGE'S FATHER

Samuel Taylor Coleridge was the youngest of the four children of whom the Reverend Coleridge was father, though as John Coleridge's second wife, Anne Bowden Coleridge brought ten children with her. Samuel is said to have been in personality most like his father, and judging from the father's interests and accomplishments, there is much reason to accept the idea. Coleridge's letters to Thomas Poole in 1797 tell much of the poet's early relationship with his father and much about his early life. The student of Coleridge who wishes to move beyond a mere outline of the poet's life should count these letters as absolutely necessary to his study. In one such letter Coleridge wrote,

My Father, (Vicar of, and Schoolmaster at, Ottery St. Mary, Devon) was a profound Mathematician, and well versed in the Latin, Greek & Oriental Languages. He published, or rather attempted to publish, several works.

My Father made the world his confidant with respect to his Learning & ingenuity: & the world seems to have kept the secret very faithfully.

The truth is, My Father was not a first-rate Genius - he was however a first-rate Christian. . . .in learning, good-heartedness, absentness of mind, & excessive ignorance of the world, he was a perfect Parson Adams.

But, two major differences in father and son appear immediately: Coleridge was not to remain ignorant of the world, and the world was not to keep a secret about his learning and ingenuity. Coleridge seems to have grown up more or less without the companionship of other children. His elder brothers were apparently not inclined toward association with him. One can speculate what this early loneliness had to do with throwing Coleridge on the resources of his own mind, with encouraging his voracious reading from an early age and promoting his use of his rich imagination for making the world into what he wanted. He spent more time to himself than with others, occasionally acting out what he read. However, Coleridge's father, not surprisingly, given the kinds of interests his father had, was an intellectual companion to him and probably made an effort to feed his son's imagination.

It was a companionship probably all too unfortunately ended by the death of the Reverend Coleridge in Samuel's ninth year. Though such speculation is ultimately pointless, one wonders if the father's hope that his son enter the Anglican ministry might not otherwise have taken a more serious turn.

COLERIDGE'S READING

It is evident in the records of Coleridge's life that he was early inclined toward wide and varied reading, and the adults who knew him affirmed his precocity through their wonderment at his astounding range and depth of conversation for a child. Coleridge is said to have found particular delight in going to his aunt's home in Crediton, because there he was able to read through her wondrous treasury of books. He was especially thrilled by the Arabian Nights, about which he later remarked, "one tale ... made so deep an impression on me ... that I was haunted by specters, whenever I was in the dark: and I distinctly recollect the anxious and fearful eagerness with which I used to watch the window in which the books lay, and whenever the sun lay upon them, I would seize it, carry it by the wall, and bask and read."

COLERIDGE'S FORMAL SCHOOLING

Coleridge's formal schooling begins soon after his father's death. He would probably have continued school at the Vicarage had it not been the case that he repeatedly came home from school hours recounting with annoyance the errors his father's successor made in grammar. It was enough to cause his mother to see the necessity of a change.

By way of a visit with his maternal uncle, John Bowden, Coleridge left for Christ's Hospital in London in April of 1782. Before Coleridge was actually enrolled, his uncle, fond of conversation and conviviality, took him along for a number of evenings in coffee houses and taverns. Coleridge, a country boy, was suddenly in the midst of the discussion of ideas and issues. He is said to have struck awe among his conversational companions - some of them becoming listeners more than companions. In his tenth year "Coleridge the Talker" had become already an established fact.

CHRIST'S HOSPITAL IN LONDON

At Christ's Hospital Coleridge passed through an initial period of loneliness, but this was soon overcome through his superlative gifts for attracting people to him. He was a young Ancient Mariner, holding listeners with the glittering eye of gripping conversation. One should be suspicious of stories about Coleridge's isolation and loneliness; some of the lines of "Frost at Midnight," the lines about his youth and what he envisions for his son, Hartley, can give the wrong impression. Indeed, Coleridge was predisposed from an early time to the writing of dejection odes that give all too melancholy an impression of his youth. Wordsworth had the capacity for withdrawing and living unto himself, making nature, and not humanity, his companion. But Coleridge was too gregarious; other persons were too important to him. Besides, one wonders with regard to the feelings and responses of other persons how really alone such a character could have been.

The importance of Coleridge's years in London should be seen clearly. Here Coleridge continued that kind of heterogeneous reading that he had shown already a passion for. He went very nearly as often as the regulations would allow to the King Street Library for his quota of books. It is said, in fact, that he read every book in the Library.

COLERIDGE'S FRIENDSHIP WITH CHARLES LAMB

One of Coleridge's most abiding friendships, that with Charles Lamb, was first established at Christ's Hospital. Coleridge's academic progress at Christ's Hospital was a rapid as might be expected, and he entered University training in 1787. A year later he came under the excellent mentorship of the Reverend James Boyer, the upper grammar master, who taught a carefully chosen group of students in Greek. Boyer once gave the description of Coleridge, the brilliant but too undisciplined student, "That sensible fool, Coleridge." E. H. Coleridge, in the best collection of Coleridge's poetry to date, *The Complete*

Poetical Works of Coleridge, gives 1787 as the year of the composition of "Easter Holidays," "Dura Navis," and "Nil Pejus est Caelibe Vita." Several of these poems, though minor poems, are worthwhile reading for the student of Coleridge's poetry. They hint at certain characteristic emphases of years to follow. Especially interesting for suggestions of later poetic directions are the fifth and sixth verses of "Easter Holidays," "Dura Navis," **stanza** three particularly of "Nil Pejus est Caelibe Vita," the "Sonnet to the Autumnal Moon" (1788), and "Life" (1789).

COLERIDGE AND MARY EVANS

The event of Coleridge's meeting with the Evans family and his subsequent relationship with them requires attention in any biographical account, if for no other reason because of the way it prepared him for his marriage to Sarah Fricker in 1795. Coleridge became romantically interested in Mary Evans almost immediately upon meeting her. She was one of three sisters in the Evans family. It seems to have been the history of the relationship that he always took her more seriously than she took him, at least in the sense of romantic love.

Coleridge said to his friend Robert Southey, "I loved her, Southey! almost to madness." Coleridge was clearly aware of Mary Evans' refusal by the end of the year 1794. It was an emotional blow that he reeled under and did not quickly recover from.

EARLY USE OF OPIUM

While in Cambridge Coleridge began to use opium, though the drug did not really become a seriously incapacitating habit until 1803, a particularly bad year for Coleridge, in which many notebook entries show evidence of both emotional and physical agony. The first accounts of Coleridge's use of opium come in 1793. Students generally hear about this problem in Coleridge's life in connection with the apologetic preface to "Kubla Khan." As will be said later in a larger consideration of the subject in the interpretation of "Kubla Khan," one should not take the opium matter with disproportionate seriousness. For all the talk about "Coleridge's failure," one should remember first that Coleridge talked more than most about his various conditions of mind and body; second, that he had more irons in the fire through his life than one can easily count, and, too that he often shows concern about the quality, or lack of quality, in what he writes; he often attempts to explain the absence of the quality that he thinks should be there by saying that such and such a poem is published because it is a kind of curiosity, not because it has any real poetic merit. Beware that preface to "Kubla Khan"! The poem was probably carefully worked at.

It should be noted that there was nothing in the use of opium at that time that would have about it the sense of alarm and suspicion that we feel today. Opium was commonly administered to patients by doctors, and one could acquire the drug without difficulty. Coleridge's rheumatic condition seems to have been the reason for his first taking opium, though it is clear that its increasing use through the years was probably more related to pain of a psychic, rather than of a strictly physical sort.

Coleridge's brothers found his expenses more alarming than any other circumstance of his life at Cambridge. He was writing to them frequent requests for money and attempting to mollify their alarm with frequent letters of reassurance to his brother George and through writing sermons for George's use in his pulpit. But the reports that such people as the Evans family gave on Coleridge's conduct made it very plain that he was spending far more time drinking, talking and carousing than he was spending in the pursuit of any kind of structured academic program. Coleridge's explanations of his activities at Cambridge were proved to be lies by the best evidence of all - his debts. No camouflage was adequate to hide them from view.

ROMANTICISM AS REVOLUTION

Less immediately inconvenient, but in some ways no less alarming than Coleridge's mounting indebtedness, was his newly formed allegiance to William Frend, a fellow of Jesus College, a dissenter from the Anglican Church and its doctrinal and liturgical orthodoxy, and a declared Unitarian. Frend's notoriety was established by the publication in 1793 of a tract bearing the title Peace and Union recommended to the Associated Bodies of Republicans and Anti-Republicans. The tract carried a serious criticism of the liturgical practices of the Church of England. Coleridge liked him and his ideas, enough in fact, to attend Frend's trial and actually cheer out loud once when a defense of Frend's positions was made. The Vice-Chancellor's Court in May, 1793 condemned Frend's ideas, convicted him of seditious acts against the State, and what then would have been the same, of defamatory acts against the Church. Frend was dismissed from the University.

Some detail about this alliance of interests with Frend is important to recognize for what it reveals of the tone and temper of the times and of Coleridge's career in Cambridge. Students of Coleridge are too much prone to skip over the facts of his practical, life-size involvements, too much inclined to miss the fact that he was a revolutionary in the time of the rising tide of political passion that we study in the two culminating national events, the American Revolution and the French Revolution. Students of Coleridge's poetry and students of the other literature of this period (even the poetry of John Keats) need to bear always in mind that Romanticism means, and perhaps means first of all, reaction; we might even get more of the spirit of the literature to say that Romanticism means rebellion - rebellion in a number of senses. Carl R. Woodring's book, *Politics in the Poetry of Coleridge*, should be read for what it reveals of the extent of Coleridge's involvements in revolutionary affairs. His book is a good account of the volcanic blasting and melting of the times.

COLERIDGE AS REVOLUTIONARY POET

The tide of reaction in Romanticism is perhaps most readily evident in the work of William Blake. In such a poem as "The Marriage of Heaven and Hell" by Blake, one finds in a relatively short work, reaction against established practices in poetic **diction**, against accepted orthodox theological concepts, and against reigning ideas about the nature of the human eye and brain. But reaction is evident in Coleridge's poetry too: it just takes a little more looking for. A fact to remember: Coleridge was certainly a poet of revolutionary spirit, not only that, but definitely that! Several problems obscure the fact: his more openly political poems are not as well known as his other works; his political prose is not read very much; to know what Coleridge's ideas were, we nearly have to settle which day we are talking about - he is not best known for consistency; what he held one day, he might modify considerably, or even renounce the next day; he did not take his revolutionary talk and writing to the ultimate conclusion of revolutionary action, the kind of action that would turn sedition into treason - there is aggressive surge, but it is mollified by passive recoil. With regard to the last factor, it is not that he loved bravery less, but probably that he loved relaxation (or just inactivity) more. Somewhere, however, the student of Coleridge should be defended in his confusion, defended by having cited the one lucid fact that Coleridge was at times such a brilliant liar. But discouragement from the study of Coleridge because of his prevarications should be checked by another lucid fact: despite his brilliance in misrepresentation, he was not usually successful in covering his tracks.

SILAS TOMKYN COMBERBACKE AND THE 15TH LIGHT DRAGOONS

Coleridge continued the sowing of financial wild oats at Cambridge, and at his brothers' expense. Economic embarrassment was the principal cause, it seems, of Coleridge's entry into what has become the one most comic experience of his life-service in the King's Regiment of the Dragoons. Coleridge was hardly suited for the life of the cavalry, not the least evidence of which was that he could not stay on a horse. The relationship with the Evans family, a source of considerable upheaval now in the continued disappointment of Coleridge's romantic hopes, probably added incentive to his enlistment. He took the nom de guerre of Silas Tomkyn Comberbacke. He was sworn into the Regiment on 4 December; by the following February he had definitely had enough. It was a time of painful re-examination of himself, a time of great guilt over the way he felt he had squandered his opportunities in the past several years, a time of stricken conscience over having to come to his brothers for release and relief.

After considerable negotiations, involving family and friends, and college officials, a discharge for Silas Tomkyn

Comberbacke was obtained the second week in April, 1794; the grounds of discharge: insanity. The whole matter, as suggested, had not been easily accomplished, and the grounds on which the discharge was granted testified to the fact. But Coleridge's sanity is quite evident in the logical plans he made for himself in the future and in the renewed practical demands for money from his brothers. Coleridge returned to Jesus College immediately upon his release.

PANTISOCRACY

During a visit with a college friend the following summer, Coleridge made the acquaintance of Robert Southey, another poet, who was to become involved in Coleridge's life in a most momentous way. Southey was to become Coleridge's brother-in-law through the passionately made plans for Pantisocracy, and was later to pick up many of the pieces of those well-laid plans in the support of Coleridge's family. At the time of their first meeting, Coleridge was 22, Southey 20. Southey was almost immediately gripped by Coleridge's commanding ideas and charming personality. The two young men felt the camaraderie of shared views on literature and politics. Coleridge, though probably less impressed with Southey than Southey was with him, would have admired the fact that Southey had stated publicly his feelings against established order and had gotten into actual trouble with authorities for it. Coleridge was also taken with Southey's zeal to put into actual practice some of the concepts of Plato's *Republic* in the establishment of a kind of ideal community. Coleridge's several experiences, academic, political, romantic (the disappointing involvement with Mary Evans), had probably much to do with preparing his mind for what Robert Southey was considering.

Pantisocracy was the name designed for the community that Coleridge, Southey, and a group of other select Englishmen planned together during the summer of 1794. The plan was to establish a community of about a dozen English families in America on the banks of the Susquehannah River. It takes no great magic of perception to determine who made up the name. Coleridge wrote it Pantocracy in a letter to Southey on 6 July 1794, a letter that bears the heading "S. T. Coleridge to R. Southey-Health & Republicanism!" Coleridge said in that letter, with regard to a man named Joseph Hucks who was traveling with him at the time, "My companion is a Man of cultivated, tho' not vigorous, understanding - his feelings are all on the side of humanity - yet such are the unfeeling Remarks, which the lingering Remains of Aristocracy occasionally prompt. When the pure System of Pantocracy shall have aspheterized the Bounties of Nature, these things will not be so - !" Coleridge also formed the word aspheterized to mean not one's very own. - In other words there would be no privately owned property in Pantisocracy. Seven days later Coleridge writes to Southey again, "I have positively done nothing but dream of the System of no Property every step of the Way since I left you - till last Sunday."

OBJECTIVES OF PANTISOCRACY

The objective in the community Pantisocracy was to come as near as possible to the elimination of greed through the abolition of private ownership. Again to Robert Southey 21 October, Coleridge writes, "Wherever Men can be vicious, some will be. The leading Idea of Pantisocracy is to make men necessarily virtuous by removing all Motives to Evil - all possible Temptations." But, as is suggested in some of Coleridge's comments, his interest in the scheme had roots in layers of reality much beyond the political and humanitarian. Besides a kind of basic personality pattern of recurrent advance and retreat throughout his life, "surge and recoil," as Carl Woodring describes it, there were all the personal factors of his life at this time that caused longing eyes and sighs after the calm of a rural setting. There brotherhood in like aims would mean common labor for a common harvest in common ownership, domestic peace, expanding knowledge, and the best environment possible for the rearing of children. It should be noted that Coleridge did not have the positive expectation of Pantisocracy that it would be the seed from which would grow the perfect society: though he was unrealistic in his failure to reckon in such a plan with the selfishness of human beings - even his own - he was not so unrealistic as to think that Pantisocracy on the banks of the Susquehannah would be the catalytic center of a miraculous millennium. Coleridge's concept emphasized more the negative approach: reduce the ownership of private property, and you will improve (not perfect) the state of man's life. It was a limited scheme, designed essentially to limit the temptation to call things one's very own.

The inventors and supporters of the pantisocratic scheme evangelized their cause, preaching this ideal form of republicanism from town to town, from crowd to crowd. Coleridge's rich, compelling conversation spellbound, as usual, his listeners. At the end of one such walking tour, which he had shared with fellow pantisocrats, Coleridge rejoined Southey in Bristol. This was in August 1794.

COLERIDGE'S INTRODUCTION TO THE FRICKER FAMILY

The one event of most far - reaching effect in Coleridge's life to come out of the enthusiasm for Pantisocracy was his meeting with the Fricker family. Southey had arranged introductions for

Coleridge to persons living in Bristol who were interested in Pantisocracy. The Fricker family were among these enthusiasts; in fact, they were the most zealous and the most concerned of the Bristol pantisocrats. Coleridge was warmly welcomed into this family of a widowed woman and her five daughters. One of the daughters, Edith, was affianced to Robert Southey; another daughter, Sarah, was to become Coleridge's wife. Pantisocracy was to begin on the banks of the Susquehannah River in America the following March. The Fricker family would join en masse. There were unattached daughters, and there were available poets. Southey was already affianced to one of the daughters, Edith. It seemed only reasonable that one of them would be right for Coleridge and that a Coleridge - Fricker marriage would be right for Pantisocracy. On the whole, though Coleridge was propelled toward the marriage by his own interest in the pantisocratic plans, and probably too by his failure with Mary Evans, the idea of marriage seems to have been more passionately supported by Southey than passionately entered into by Coleridge.

When Coleridge returned to Cambridge in September, Southey was not long in remonstrating him for his neglect of his correspondence with Sarah Fricker.

It is clear from several pieces of strong evidence that Coleridge had not really recovered from his disappointment with Mary Evans. His memory of her, as his letters to Southey during these latter months of 1794 reveal, was still fresh, too fresh for him to be at ease with the plans that had been made for his marriage with Sarah Fricker. It was a time of confusion and upheaval, but still a time of energetic and productive intellectual activity.

EARLY POLITICAL POEMS

A number of political poems were published by the *Morning Chronicle* during December and January, including the following **Sonnets** on Eminent Characters: "Burke," "Priestley," "Koskiuski," "Godwin," "Southey" and "Sheridan." Coleridge in the midst of all the emotional turmoil still made a name for himself as a political rebel. In Bristol he gave a number of lectures on political subjects. Pitt was a frequent target. The lecture series was a part of a plan decided on by Coleridge and Southey to make a living through literary endeavor. There was not only the immediate problem of earning daily bread, but there was also the problem of building up some financial reserve looking toward the emigration to America in March. Coleridge's subjects, political and theological, included "An Address to the People, against Ministerial Treason." In politics Coleridge voiced opposition to the slave trade, opposition to war, opposition, consequently, to the policies of William Pitt, opposition to the ministerial defense of war against France as an act of Christian Faith. The lectures brought Coleridge friendships with Unitarians and their support; the lectures brought him opposition from aristocrats and at least one accusation of treason.

COLERIDGE'S MEETING WITH JOSEPH COTTLE

In Bristol, Coleridge was blessed with the formation of friendship with Joseph Cottle. Cottle was a bookseller by trade, a practitioner in poetry, an ardent supporter of young poets. One has only to look at Coleridge's letters to Cottle to recognize the extent of his kind support of Coleridge, often beyond the call of publishing duty. Cottle favored Coleridge and Southey with energetic and faithful encouragement. The two poets received from him money, favors, advertisement, promised publication. For all of Cottle's interest and help, and for all of their shared interest in Pantisocracy, Coleridge's stay in Bristol was a time of divisions and increasing divisions between Southey and himself. The more practical Southey wrote in a systematic, disciplined manner; the more undisciplined, though ultimately more productive, Coleridge wrote in a more "turning, and twisting, and winding, and doubling" way. Southey considered more pragmatic plans for Pantisocracy; Coleridge talked passionately along the original idealistic lines. The two men grew wider apart. Perhaps Southey too presumptuously appointed himself for the reform of Coleridge's character.

MARRIAGE AND RESIDENCE AT CLEVEDON

When Coleridge rented a cottage at Clevedon on the Bristol Channel in August, 1795, looking toward his marriage, the original dream of Pantisocracy had pretty much faded away. The original group of enthusiasts had dispersed. Coleridge wrote to Southey in early August, 1795, "Southey! Pantisocracy is not the Question - it's realization is distant - perhaps a miraculous Millennium-"

It is possible that the rupture between Coleridge and Southey and the resulting gossip that spread through a part of Bristol about the failure of pantisocratic hope hastened the marriage of Coleridge and Sarah Fricker. Joseph Cottle came to the newly-married Coleridges with help, fraternal and financial. He offered Coleridge a salary for regular productions of poetry and prose. But the Clevedon residence was not to have a lasting appeal.

BACK TO BRISTOL AND THE WATCHMAN

Coleridge's residence at Clevedon was made unforgettable by his composition there of "The Eolian Harp." The poem seems to speak joyfully of his life there with his new wife, though it probably reveals upon closer reading a number of tensions, political, theological, perhaps ever marital. The degree of real joy and contentment at Clevedon, whatever it was, was not sufficient to keep the Coleridges much over a month. The husband was probably the more discontent of the two; he missed the Bristol Library and the intellectual excitement of the city. Another scheme, having truth and freedom as basic principles, came into existence at this point. This scheme was more literary than communal, however, and it added the possibility of financial returns to the implementation of a noble cause.

The Watchman was born at Rummer Tavern in Bristol in December, 1795. The first issue was to be distributed on Friday, 5 February 1796. The emphases of the publication were to be mainly political, as the announcements about its contents made known to prospective readers. The motto read, "That all may know the Truth;/ And that the Truth may make us Free!!" The principal objectives of *The Watchman* were, "to cooperate (1) with the Whig Club in procuring a repeal of Lord Grenville's and Mr. Pitt's bills, now passed into laws, and (2) with the Patriotic Societies for obtaining a Right of Suffrage general and frequent." *The Watchman* would, then, "proclaim the State of the Political Atmosphere, and preserve Freedom and her Friends from the attacks of Robbers and Assassins!!" But the citizenry of Bristol did not respond with interest sufficient to the needs of the publication. Coleridge consequently undertook a tour of Birmingham, Nottingham, Sheffield, Manchester, Liverpool and Litchfield in order to enlist subscribers. During the tour he preached often in Unitarian churches. Years later, Coleridge gave an interesting account of his travels and experiences in the *Biographia Literaria*.

FAILURE OF THE WATCHMAN

The Watchman all too quickly ran the same course of a number of Coleridge's involvements. Begun in March it had too much of the proverbial character of the month: coming in like a lion, going out like a lamb. More precisely, *The Watchman*, after steady declines in popularity and subscribers, had no detectable pulse after 13 May. The weeks following the failure of *The Watchman* were more vexing financially. Coleridge's life became complicated by additional concerns: his wife was more often sick than well; he now had another mouth to feed, for his first son, David Hartley, was born in September; he was writing more now for bread than for joy. Cottle, in fact, had already paid him for poems he had not yet written.

POEMS PUBLISHED

Coleridge's most continued labor during these days was "Religious Musings," a longer poem heavy with theological and political thought. Coleridge spoke of the extreme labor that he put in on the poem: "I torture the poem and myself with corrections." "Religious Musings" was published in a collection of Coleridge's poems called Poems on Various Subjects in April of 1796, a volume that contained the shorter poems, "The Eolian Harp," "Songs of the Pixies," and "Lines Written at Shurton Bars." The shorter poems were to find their way to the more frequented shelf of English poetry than the laboriously written and rewritten "Religious Musings." But the longer poem remains an important record of Coleridge's thought during the years, 1794, 1795, and 1796. Any serious student of Coleridge's poetry should fix extended attention on it.

(For a survey of the events of Coleridge's life from this point to December of 1798, see the Introduction and Biographical Context for "*The Rime of the Ancient Mariner.*")

COLERIDGE'S ANNUS MIRABILIS

The refusal in December of 1798 of Coleridge's tragedy *Osorio* for performance at Drury Lane renewed his financial worries and his fear that he would not be able to earn a living through his writing. Daniel Stuart of the *Morning Post* offered him a writing assignment, regular contributions of poetry and prose for regular money. But it was not enough; he had to look for other employment.

THE UNITARIAN MINISTRY AS POSSIBLE VOCATION

He began about this time a serious consideration of the Unitarian ministry. He would preach some Sundays at Shrewsbury to see how he felt about preaching for pay. This consideration became intensified at Christmas with an offer from John P. Estlin, Unitarian minister and friend of Coleridge. He would recommend Coleridge for the soon-to-be-vacated pulpit at Shrewsbury.

Another possibility presented itself. The mail on Christmas Day brought an offer of a gift of money from Josiah Wedgwood, an admirer or Coleridge's abilities and accomplishments. The gift of one-hundred pounds from Wedgwood was designed to free Coleridge from the financial worries that were pressing him into the acceptance of a position that might very well prove incompatible with his principles, and a position that would leave him no time, or little time, for the cultivation of his talents. In the midst of great fluctuation of mind about the offer, Coleridge returned the money to Wedgwood on 5 January 1798.

COLERIDGE'S MEETING OF WILLIAM HAZLITT

After these struggles with himself about the Wedgwood offer, Coleridge went to Shrewsbury to succeed the Reverend John Rowe as minister of the Unitarian Church there. The visit that Coleridge paid to that congregation was the occasion for one of the best known descriptions of him, that of William Hazlitt in "My First Acquaintance with Poets."

THE WEDGWOOD ANNUITY

On 10 January 1798 the Wedgwoods made another offer to Coleridge, this time an annuity, "an annuity of 150f for life . . . no condition whatever being annexed." Thomas Poole strongly admonished Coleridge to accept the offer. This time, persuaded of the rightness of acceptance, Coleridge on 19 January declined candidacy for the Shrewsbury charge. Writing to J. P. Estlin on 16 January, Coleridge clarified that his refusal of the pulpit at Shrewsbury did not in any way mean a change of personal faith and intention regarding his labor in the name of "Christianity & practical Religion."

THE POEMS OF THE ANNUS MIRABILIS

Coleridge's annus mirabilis, 1797-1798, the "wonderful year," probably owes something to his having been freed from bread-winning. The early part of this year, 1798, rather than the whole of the year, saw him writing the poems for which he is best known. During February he composed "France: an Ode," and "Frost at Midnight." In March he finished "The Ancient Mariner." April was the month of "Fears of Solitude" and "The Nightingale." This was probably the time also for the writing of "Kubla Khan," though there is division of opinion about the date of that poem. It was a time of closeness and rich companionship with the Wordsworths. It would be difficult to find a period of Coleridge's life that shows a comparable degree of personal happiness. Dorothy Wordsworth's Journal was first kept during these months, January to March, and the student of Coleridge should not miss her day by day account of the life Coleridge and the Wordsworths became absorbed in during this time.

STUDY AND TRAVEL IN GERMANY

By March of 1798 Coleridge and the Wordsworths had arrived at a kind of design for a trip to Germany; at least the scheme was in agitation by that time. One of Wordsworth's letter from the second week in March indicates that the purposes of the trip were to be intellectual: "We have come to a resolution, Coleridge, Mrs. Coleridge, my Sister, and myself of going into Germany, where was purpose to pass the two ensuing years in order to acquire the German language, and to furnish ourselves with a tolerable stock of information in natural science. Our plan is to settle, if possible, in a village near a University, in a pleasant, and if we can a mountainous, country; it will be desirable that the place should be as near as may be to Hamburg, on account of the expense of travelling." Dorothy, writing to Richard Wordsworth on 30 April, specified the other main objective of the journey," . . . translation is the most profitable of all works." Coleridge had long been interested in translation; he tells in a letter of 5 May 1796, addressed to Thomas Poole, that he has been studying German and that he has had thoughts of suggesting to a London bookseller that he go to Jena where Schiller resided and translate all of Schiller's works. In return, the bookseller would pay for the trip. With respect to Coleridge's participation in the travels to Germany, more needs to be said, for the sojourn there for him had causes that were related in a serious and encompassing way to his poetic development. In a letter to Joseph Cottle in early April, 1797, a letter in which Coleridge brings his astute critical powers to bear on the work of Robert Southey, he speaks of his own ambitions as a poet. In a context of praise of Milton as a poet, he speaks of what he would consider necessary in his own preparation for writing an **epic** poem:

> "Observe the march of Milton - his severe application, his laborious polish, his deep metaphysical researches, his prayers to God before he began his great poem, all that could lift and swell his intellect, became his daily food. I should not think of devoting less than 20 years to an Epic Poem. Ten to collect materials and warm my mind with universal science. I would be a tolerable Mathematician, I would thoroughly know Mechanics, Hydrostatics, Optics, and Astronomy, Botany, Metallurgy, Fossilism, Chemistry, Geology, Anatomy, Medicine - then mind of man - then the minds of men - in all Travels, Voyages and Histories. So I would spend ten years - the next five to the composition of the poem - and the five last to the correction of it.

So I would write haply not unhearing of that divine and rightly - whispering Voice, which speaks to mighty minds of predestinated Garlands, starry and unwithering."

One may find repeated statements of ambition such as this throughout Coleridge's letters and notebooks. It seems not presumptuous to associate such grandiose aspiration with his failure to write no more poetry than he did. (There has been much lamenting of Cole idge's failure as a poet, though no one really knows what success and failure in these terms mean; we seem to regret that he did not write more poems like "The Ancient Mariner.") There was in Coleridge the desire to write at some time the great encyclopedic work on human knowledge and human life. He spoke sometimes of the Logosophia, his one grand and definitive work. But, it seems the case that the higher Coleridge schemed of master plans, the less capable he became of them, not to say the more anxiety-ridden.

Clearly, Coleridge's interest in the expedition to Germany was far more than a casual desire to travel for culture. The ever-restless intellectual curiosity of his mind gave the project of traveling to and studying in Germany an intensity that was not really shared by Wordsworth. The interest of the Wordsworths was more in viewing the countryside. When they separated from each other during the time they were away from England, it was probably more because Coleridge wished to settle in and study, and the Wordsworths wished to tour.

Coleridge was first at Ratzeburg, where his popularity became soon established, then in February in Göttingen, where it was said about him by one of his frequent conversationalists, "Coleridge is much liked notwithstanding many peculiarities. He is very liberal towards all doctrines and opinions and cannot be put out of temper. . . ." Another part of his companion's statement is true to what was said so often about him, in one way or another: "The great fault which his friends lament is the variety of subjects which he adopts, and the too abstruse nature of his ordinary speculations. . . ."

ACCOMPLISHMENTS IN GERMANY

But talk did not replace work. Alice D. Snyder published in Modern Philology an impressive list of Coleridge's reading in Göttingen. He read Kant some, though not seriously. There is in Clement Carlyon's *Early Years and Late Reflections* a humorous story of Coleridge's conversing with a German girl about the philosophy of Kant and her being stunned to recognize that Coleridge understood in German what she could not. When Coleridge left Germany in July of 1799, he left without having accomplished the literary works that he had intended. But this should not in any way eclipse the importance of his stay there for his intellectual growth. He had remained in that country for eleven months. He had been homesick, severely so at times, as his letters show. And during the time he had suffered the news of his infant's death; he learned in March that Berkeley, his second son, had died 10 February. Generally his wife's letter to him had been none too encouraging. Still he had done a great deal. One may speculate, though it is speculation, that the greatest single result of the time spent in Germany was a shift in Coleridge's basic literary interests away from the kind of poetry that "The Ancient Mariner," "Christabel," and "Kubla Khan" represent to works more philosophical, more theological. In making such a speculation one recalls some lines from a poem written in Coleridge's later life: in "The Garden of Boccaccio" he was to write in 1828, a half dozen years before his death, that poetry had really been philosophy:

"And last, a matron now, of sober mien,
Yet radiant still and with no earthly sheen,
Whom as a faery child my childhood woo'd
Even in my dawn of thought - Philosophy,
Though then unconscious of herself, pardie,
She bore no other name than Poesy...."

KANT'S WORKS

Somewhat ironically the one German philosopher who was to have the most gripping, profound, and abiding influence on Coleridge was not that seriously read by him in Germany; Kant's works came home in Coleridge's box of "**metaphysical**" books, the pages of those works mostly unread and unmarked.

(For a survey of the events of Coleridge's life from this point through the time of his writing "Dejection: An Ode," see the Introduction and Biographical Context for that poem.)

BEYOND DEJECTION

Although our survey of Coleridge's life concludes with the events surrounding his writing of "Dejection: An Ode," there are a number of reasons for taking the remainder of his years just as seriously. Indeed, some students of his work never study him that seriously as a poet during the years covered in this biographical record. He is after 1802 to have many important involvements, to do much significant work, to leave much deep influence in literary criticism and theology. But, since this study is of Coleridge's poetry, the events of his life after 1802 do not concern us as seriously as the events before that year, for after that time the waters of Hippocrene become more or less unavailable to him; he does not write any more really great poetry. He occasionally turns out some good lines; there are some occasional strong reminders of the Coleridge of the *Conversation Poems*, of "Dejection," even an echo from time to time of those enchanting sounds of the three magical poems. But, no more truly great poetry. Of the later poems, "To William Wordsworth" (1807), and "The Garden of Boccaccio" (1828) are probably most interesting. After 1802 Coleridge is spellbinding conversationalist; lecturer (sometimes brilliant, sometimes unintelligible); critic on literature, politics, society, current events; playwright; drug addict, occasionally a poet; philosopher and theologian of lasting significance. Whatever Xanadu was for him, he never found it again, perhaps mainly because he did not want to, perhaps because it was a place that no one could really endure for that long.

REMAINING YEARS OF COLERIDGE'S LIFE

1804 - 1806: Coleridge lived in Malta and the area of the Mediterranean, mainly for the purpose of recovering his health. He worked during the time as "diplomatic under-strapper" to the Governor of Malta. He returned to England in worse health than he suffered when he left, more addicted than ever to opium.

1808: The year of the first course of lectures on literature in the Royal Institution in London.

1809: Began *The Friend*, a weekly paper, concerned with "literary, moral, political" matters; it appeared irregularly between the months of June, 1809 and March, 1810, for a total of twenty-seven issues. The material of the paper was published later in 1812 as a book.

1810: Coleridge and Wordsworth suffered alienation through a misunderstanding perpetrated by Basil Montagu.

Wordsworth had made a remark about Coleridge's personal habits, but it was received by Coleridge differently than it had been intended by Wordsworth.

1813: The revision of Coleridge's drama *Osorio*, played under the title of Remorse, but only with moderate success.

1813 - 1816: The year of the beginning of Coleridge's *Biographia Literaria*, a rambling and confusing work, but probably as important as any single work on literature in English. Lectured on Shakespeare in Bristol (brilliant but disjointed Shakespearean criticism). Coleridge put himself under the care of Dr. Gillman at Highgate and intended to stay for a month. He was to live with Dr. Gillman the rest of his life. Published "Christabel."

1817: Year of the publication of: *Lay Sermons, Biographia Literaria, Sibylline Leaves, Zapolya*. Attacked harshly by William Hazlitt.

1818 - 1823: Continued to lecture and began to develop a following in such persons as J. H. Green, Thomas Allsop and John Sterling. The beginning of the work that was to earn him veneration as the "Oracle of Highgate."

1825: The year of the publication of *Aids to Reflection*, a work of theological nature that was to have an abiding influence in the development of English theology, especially the Oxford Movement.

1830: Year of the publication of *Constitution of Church and State*.

1834: Year of Coleridge's death, on 25 July.

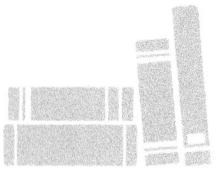

THE RIME OF THE ANCIENT MARINER

INTRODUCTION

COLERIDGE MEETS WILLIAM WORDSWORTH

Among the waves that gathered forcefully, broke loudly and retreated quietly through Coleridge's correspondence of May, 1796, there is the tumult of uncertain vocational directions: translating Schiller, tutoring, preaching. But there is the high-water mark of enthusiasm during the year of meeting a young poet by the name of William Wordsworth; the friendship would leave a high-water mark on English poetry.

From the many sources of information we have of their associations, there is no doubting the importance of their shared enthusiasms about poetry, their searching conversations, and their actual cooperation in the production of poetic works. However, stating that their agreements were many and profound does not mean that there were not some basic areas in which they did disagree, and disagree profoundly. Some of the disagreement can be felt in Coleridge's criticism in his *Biographia Literaria* of Wordsworth's poetry. Coleridge and Wordsworth were often together during the months of what has come to be known as Coleridge's annus mirabilis, the time during which "*The Rime of the Ancient Mariner*" was written.

THE MOVE TO NETHER STOWEY

Through the year 1796 Coleridge continued preaching, he wrote reviews and articles, he had a moment of renewed interest in *The Watchman*, he nearly became private tutor to the two young sons of a Mrs. Evans, he was tempted by the idea of starting a school for a dozen pupils, he agreed to being mentor to Charles Lloyd. One strategic decision of the year was that Coleridge would move near to a substantial, learned man by the name of Thomas Poole. Poole lived at Nether Stowey; Nether Stowey was near Alfoxden where the Wordsworths were to live. Coleridge had first met Thomas Poole in August of 1794 during the evangelizing of Pantisocracy. Coleridge had greatly admired this generous gentleman, who though denied the rights of university education had seen to his own intellectual growth during the hours that he had free from his various business commitments. However temperamentally unsuited Coleridge was for it, he admired Poole's efficient handling of manual labor. Besides, the effective combination of work with the hands, and intellectual and spiritual development would in Coleridge's scheme of interests far outlast the demise of Pantisocracy. Poole expressed some misgiving about the move, but finally agreed. Coleridge moved to Nether Stowey, which was near the Quantock Hills, and near the towns of Bristol and Taunton, where Coleridge continued to preach. And the Wordsworth, William and his sister Dorothy, returned to Nether Stowey with Coleridge in early July. A walking tour from which Coleridge was excluded because of an injury to his foot was the occasion during this time for his writing "This Lime-Tree Bower my Prison."

THE WORDSWORTHS MOVE NEAR COLERIDGE

The best evidence for the quick and moving friendship that Coleridge and the Wordsworths had formed is the fact that the Wordsworths soon moved from Racedown, forty miles away, to Alfoxden, only three miles from Nether Stowey. They all shared equal enthusiasm about the location in new quarters. During the time Coleridge and the Wordsworths had spent together, they had talked poetry and read poetry. Coleridge had been working on a tragedy, *Osorio*, during the time that Wordsworth had been writing The Borderers. They enjoyed walking tours together, interestingly reported by Dorothy Wordsworth in her Journal. The Wordsworths preferred the area to Racedown. The Quantock Hills were a source of continual delight. Coleridge's notebooks show a quickening of interest in his natural surroundings, though his accounts of landscape are probably more the product of disciplined, even dutiful observation and recording than the more spontaneous ones of Dorothy Wordsworth. But despite the probability that he was often looking for that in nature that it had become in English landscape poetry the style to find, and was probably therefore more compulsive about observing and describing natural scenery, he and the Wordsworths were all likely genuinely looking, as his poem "This Lime - Tree Bower my Prison" has it, for "religious meanings in the forms of nature." They all shared a deep interest in natural scenery. There is good reason to believe that this interest, fostered by the uncannily accurate, even microscopic eye of Dorothy Wordsworth, was one of the main reasons for Wordsworth's recovery from his disillusionment with the way in which the French Revolution had failed to fulfill the hopes of man. She called his attention to a new universe of detail in the surrounding world. From Dorothy Wordsworth Coleridge also learned a great deal about how to look at nature. His new friendship with Coleridge was the second principal means of Wordsworth's rehabilitation.

MUTUAL INFLUENCE BETWEEN WORDSWORTH AND COLERIDGE

There is some question whether Coleridge was as profoundly influenced by Wordsworth as Wordsworth was by Coleridge. One reading Wordsworth's Prelude hears numerous echoes of Coleridge's voice. Coleridge certainly lacked Wordsworth's capacity for singleness of focus, but he no doubt possessed the more comprehensive, seminal mind. Though capable of more sustained concentration on a single task, Wordsworth did not possess either the prodigious memory or the extent of reading that was Coleridge's. A book about Wordsworth patterned after J. L. Lowes' *The Road to Xanadu* would probably be half the size. Of Coleridge Wordsworth said that his was "the power . . . of throwing out in profusion grand central truths from which might be evolved the most comprehensive systems."

THE LYRICAL BALLADS

The most permanently famous literary result of the Coleridge - Wordsworth association was the planning and publication of the "Lyrical Ballads". We can assume that the essentials of the work had not only germinated but had come to considerable fruition by the last months of 1797. The association of the two men had apparently already yielded three-hundred lines of Coleridge's "Ancient Mariner" in November of that year. On 5 November Coleridge wrote to his publisher, Joseph Cottle, "I have written a **ballad** of about 300 lines."

PLANNING OF "THE ANCIENT MARINER"

The poem had been planned by Coleridge and Wordsworth during a walking tour that the poets shared in November. They were planning to write the poem together; its publication was intended to help pay the expenses of their excursion. Coleridge soon took over the writing of the poem, incorporating only a few of Wordsworth's suggestions. It turned out to be the kind of poem that Coleridge could do best.

PUBLICATION OF "THE ANCIENT MARINER"

The early months of the following year, 1798, were occupied with further planning of the *Lyrical Ballads*. The Wordsworths went to Bristol in June to make the final arrangements for the publication. The work was published anonymously in September, containing four poems by Coleridge, "The Ancient Mariner," "The Foster-Mother's Tale," "The Dungeon," and "The Nightingale," and nineteen poems by Wordsworth. The work, plainly an experimentation in poetic subject matter and poetic **diction**, seeking "to ascertain how far the language of conversation in the middle and lower classes of society is adapted to the purposes of poetic pleasure," opened with Coleridge's "Ancient Mariner" and closed with Wordsworth's "Tintern Abbey." Some people date the beginning of the Romantic Period in English Literature from the publication of the volume. This is going too far, but there is no denying the work a central place in the movement.

INFLUENCE OF THE LYRICAL BALLADS

With regard to the former established practices in the use of meter in poetry, Coleridge's and Wordsworth's innovations were serious and of far-reaching consequence. The poetry of the eighteenth-century generally has used an even meter, with a definite, specific number of syllables in each line of the poem. The line had a regular beat; this kind of poetry was not based on stress or rhythm. In the poems of the *Lyrical **Ballads*** Coleridge and Wordsworth varied freely the number of syllables and the placement of the accent in the line. The result of this kind of nearly revolutionary change in poetic metrics was that their poems had a kind of elastic quality, a quality of the spontaneous, a freedom of movement that created the effect of involvement in the things of ordinary life. The liquid movement of the meter spilled over into and affected the poetic figures and subject matter in the poems.

The volume was greeted with little praise, indeed, mostly blame. It was certainly not greeted as the parent of a new age in English poetry. The statements made by Coleridge's wife, though colored somewhat by her own hostilities, are more truthful than not truthful about the reception given *Lyrical Ballads*: "The *Lyrical Ballads* are laughed at and disliked by all with very few excepted"; "The *Lyrical **Ballads*** are not liked at all by any."

TEXTUAL ARRANGEMENT AND REARRANGEMENT

In the first publication of *"The Rime of the Ancient Mariner"* in the *Lyrical Ballads*, 1798, the following was printed in advertisement of the poem:

The Rime of the Ancyent Marinere was professedly written in imitation of the style, as well as of the spirit of the elder poets; but with a few exceptions, the Author believes that the language adopted in it has been equally intelligible for these three last centuries.

The poem was meticulously revised for the 1800 edition of the *Lyrical Ballads*. The revisions consisted of the elimination of a number of words considered too archaic, the dropping of about forty lines and the addition of a few. The title in the 1800 edition was reworded "The Ancient Mariner, A Poet's Reverie." The text of *"The Rime of the Ancient Mariner"* that appears in anthologies and collections of Coleridge's poetry is the final revision that he made in 1834 for his *Poetical Works*. This text shows a few modifications beyond those that he had made for previous editions of his poetry.

Before he begins reading the poem, the student should refresh his mind of the statements made by Coleridge in the *Biographia Literaria* about the publication of the *Lyrical Ballads*. Though his statement in the Biographia is probably enriched and expanded somewhat by the passage of about twenty years, it gives a valuable account of Coleridge's feelings respecting the new kind of poetry that he and Wordsworth were trying to write. The friendship that began between the two men in 1797, with its rich discussions of the purposes and directions of poetry, brought them to the decision to write and publish a volume of poetry in which they would abandon the traditional techniques and subject matter of 18th century verse in order to offer forceful sincerity and elemental human emotions. For them the two cardinal points of poetry were articulated in the following statement:

. . .the power of exciting the sympathy of the reader by a faithful adherence to the truth of nature, and the power of giving the interest of novelty by the modifying colors of imagination.

In this idea originated the plan of the *Lyrical Ballads*; in which it was agreed, that my [Coleridge's] endeavors should be directed to persons and characters supernatural, or at least romantic; yet so as to transfer from our inward nature a human interest and a semblance of truth sufficient to procure for these shadows of imagination that willing suspension of disbelief for the moment, which constitutes poetic faith.

In other words, Coleridge's particular task in the poems that he wrote for the *Lyrical **Ballads*** (including "*The Rime of the Ancient Mariner*") was to make credible the supernatural and wonderful.

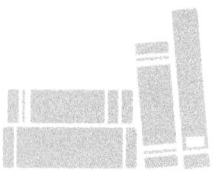

THE RIME OF THE ANCIENT MARINER

TEXTUAL ANALYSIS

PART I

A young man is singled out from a trio of gallants going to a wedding; he is next of kin to the bridegroom. The person who arrests him is the ancient Mariner. The Mariner has a story of his own experience, tragic and joyous experience, that he must tell. As the Mariner explains in Part VII of the poem, "I pass, like night, from land to land; / I have strange power of speech; / That moment that his face I see, / I know the man that must hear me: / To him my tale I teach."

The Mariner first holds this Wedding-Guest with his "skinny hand," but then the grasp of the hand is replaced by the hypnotic grasp of the Mariner's "glittering eye." The Wedding-Guest protests four times in Part I the Mariner's obstructing his attendance at the wedding. His protest centers around the fact that the wedding is an occasion of joy. Observe: "The guests are met, the feast is set . . ."; "the merry din"; the sound of "the loud bassoon"; "The bride hath paced into the hall, / Red as a rose is she; / Nodding their heads before her goes / The merry minstrelsy." But, because of the Mariner's power over him, the Wedding-Guest (**stanza** five) must swap his place at the feast for a stone.

The narrative actually begins in **stanza** four, but it is not until stanza eleven that the Mariner can continue his story without the interruption of the Wedding-Guest. The Wedding-Guest's last protest against the Mariner's tyranny over him comes in **stanza** ten. The details of the story before this time are that "There was a ship" (this is the way the Mariner begins) that left its home harbor and set a southern course toward the Line. **Stanza** seven clarifies the direction through reference to the places of the sunrise and the sunset. In **stanza** eleven the Mariner tells how a "tyrannous" wind, a "Storm Blast," in fact, drives the ship toward the south pole. The **simile** Coleridge uses in **stanza** twelve to describe the response of the ship to the propelling wind has the ominous about it: "As who pursued with yell and blow / Still treads the shadow of his foe. . . ."

Stanza 13: Mist, snow, cold, and ice greet the ship. One may get an ambiguous impression of the ice: Coleridge first describes it as "green as emerald," a positive description, for green is a favorite color with Coleridge. But then the sounds it makes seem hardly positive: "It cracked and growled, and roared and howled. . . ." The words of the gloss are: "This land of ice, and of fearful sounds where no living thing was to be seen."

Stanza sixteen introduces the bird of good omen in the poem, the Albatross, a great, white sea bird. The crew of the ship had to this point seen no signs of life, no "shapes of men nor beasts." Their loneliness would promote their welcome of the Albatross. "At length did cross an Albatross, / Thorough [sic] the fog it came; / As if it had been a Christian soul, / We hailed it in God's name." This is the first conspicuously religious event in the poem, though one could think of the wedding as having religious meaning. The crew feeds the Albatross, and the bird proves to be associated with the ship's good fortune; the **stanza** that comes immediately after the one that tells of the crew's welcome to the Albatross relates that the helmsman steered the ship safely through the ice.

Stanza eighteen follows: the wind here, formerly an ambiguous force, becomes the "good south wind." Within all of these beneficent circumstances, the Albatross comes for the companionship of food and play. Coleridge is steadily, deliberately building to the first principal point of action in the poem, the killing of the Albatross. Before getting to that last **stanza**, let the reader note carefully the build-up of the impression of goodness in the universe. In **stanza** nineteen, next to the last stanza in this part, the whiteness of the fog and the whiteness of the moonshine are blended with the whiteness of the Albatross. But, in the midst of goodness and in the midst of whiteness, all of a sudden we are told the startling news that the Mariner with his cross-bow "shot the Albatross." The Mariner's face registers extreme shock at his own alarming deed. Observe the element of contrast in the last three **stanzas** in Part I, particularly between the eighteenth and twentieth stanzas:

And a good south wind sprung up behind; The Albatross did follow, And every day, for food or play. Came to the mariners' hollo!

In mist or cloud, on mast or shroud, It perched for vespers nine; Whiles all the night, through fog-smoke white, Glimmered the white moon-shine."

"God save thee, ancient Mariner! From the fiends, that plague thee thus! - Why look'st thou so?" - "With my cross-bow I shot the Albatross.

Comment

There is no explanation at all given of why the Mariner chooses the person that he does to hear his story. In fact, the poem is full of actions and events that are left unexplained; indeed, one can say that a principal **theme** in "*The Rime of the Ancient Mariner*" is the ambiguity and ultimate mysteriousness of motive. The central crime of the poem, the Mariner's killing of the Albatross, is a crime capriciously committed.

Discussions of this poem sometimes include reference to the Wedding - Guest as the normal man, the ancient Mariner as the abnormal, and the sea - journey as symbolic of the outcast. Captain Ahab of Herman Melville's *Moby Dick* comes immediately to mind. The Mariner is certainly not tempted by the joyful noise of the wedding; his obsession to tell his story leaves him unreceptive to any other persuasion. But the Wedding-Guest does not really want to hear. No right-feeling person wishes to miss joy. The second of the interpretive comments given as the gloss in Part I tells of the power of the Mariner's eye; that "glittering eye" is mentioned three times in the first five stanzas. One is reminded of the way Geraldine's eye has the power of binding Christabel. The Mariner's power is so strong that the Wedding-Guest listens "like a three year's child." Christabel is made submissive also, even childlike, by Geraldine's power over her. There are glittering, flashing eyes in many of Coleridge's poems. The young poet in "Kubla Khan" would strike awe in his subjects, those who see him build the dome in air, and partly because of his flashing eyes.

Now, of course, if the Ancient Mariner is really a poet, then we would not expect him to put joy above other concerns; we would expect his inspiration to be the most compelling force in his life, whether it led him into what we more normal, more mortally bound creatures call joy or not. The Mariner tells the Wedding-Guest in Part VII that "this soul" [the Mariner's own soul] hath been / Alone on a wide wide sea: / So lonely 'twas, that God himself / Scarce seemed there to be." The poet is the being of all beings who sees strange sights and hears strange music. If we are ever confronted with one, we may well wonder if he is not a spirit, as the Wedding-Guest does of the Mariner, or we may even behave like those who are confronted with the dome - building youth in "Kubla Khan" - we may call him demon-possessed and try to rid him of the demon. But, of course our dilemma is always that in hearing poets we do not really know whether they are demon-possessed or inspired by God! And it is risky business to chalk off divine inspiration as a demonic curse.

Wind is often talked about in Coleridge's poems as a storm, and wind throughout his poetry has very ambiguous qualities. We may recall the way wind has been traditionally associated with inspiration. The reader of "*The Rime of the Ancient Mariner*" may find it interesting to compare the sounds that Coleridge hears in the wind in "Dejection: An Ode"; the wind is both coveted and feared by the poet who listens. He calls it a "Mighty Poet," but he hears in it sounds of fright, failure and agony.

The final **stanzas** in Part I tell of mutually harmonious relationships between man and the universe in which he lives. In these lines Coleridge is giving us a description of life in a universe where natural forces favor human welfare. The bond of relationship is even given the depth and significance of the dimension of religious faith: the Albatross participates in the evening prayers of the crew, whether "In mist or cloud, on mast or shroud."

Three sources of whiteness are juxtaposed in **stanza** nineteen: that of the fog, that of the moon-shine, that of the Albatross. White has been traditionally associated with purity, though we have known since Herman Melville's White Whale, if we did not know before, that the hue is ambivalent to the human mind, that the purity somehow lacks absolute purity. The blackness of human motive and human deed is set within the whiteness of nature and its benevolent forces, but then in a larger sense the juxtaposition of white and the black introduces the larger question of whether nature is any more benevolent than man. It is one of the principal **metaphysical** questions raised by the poem.

But immediately after the mention of vespers comes a prayer for the Mariner, certainly demon-possessed, certainly plagued by fiends. The nature of the demons is not expressed - they are just there, and the Mariner for one does not begin to understand them. Indeed, he is appalled at himself, at his own act. As one who has read "Kubla Khan" will remember, persons even yearn sometimes for demon lovers. "God save thee, ancient Mariner!" Is Coleridge suggesting that man's salvation must come from outside himself?

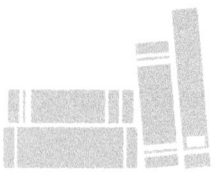

THE RIME OF THE ANCIENT MARINER

TEXTUAL ANALYSIS

PART II

The ship proceeding south from England sails around the Cape. The direction of the ship has changed at the beginning of Part II. The first **stanza** of this part tells us of the change in direction by reference to the crew's changed relationship to the rising and setting Sun: "The Sun now rose upon the right: / Out of the sea came he, / Still hid in mist, and on the left / Went down into the sea." It was not an uncommon course for ships. Coleridge would have known from his vast readings in travel literature that many ships took this route. He gives in the "Argument" the essentials of the directions of the voyage. After the ship is pushed southward by a strong wind toward the south pole and passes through the fields of ice, it sails northward again into the Pacific Ocean and reaches the Line once more. The ship, therefore, is at the Equator twice, crossing it once while sailing south through the Atlantic, and crossing it again on the northward route. The ship, of course, is becalmed at the Equator after it has come into the Pacific Ocean.

With regard to the route of the ship's travel, it is perhaps important to note, though perhaps too obvious to need mention, that the reader's expectations are sharpened by having a good half of the action of the tale take place in the Pacific, in the second part of the voyage. Think of the difference in the pace of the poem if the ship had been stopped on the southern passage.

The second **stanza** of this Part notes the absence of the Albatross but the continuance of the "good south wind." The crew, even the Mariner, regrets the loss of the "sweet bird."

Stanza three points up the extent of the Mariner's guilt: ". . . I had done a hellish thing. . . ." The Mariner becomes the object of the crew's ridicule and accusation, for they take it as a portent that he had killed the Albatross.

And I had done a hellish thing, And it would work 'em woe: For all averred, I had killed the bird That made the breeze to blow. Ah wretch! said they, the bird to slay That made the breeze to blow!

It is certainly nothing new in literature that one would be accused of a crime of deepest stain - even by oneself - if one had murdered a form of life that had offered hospitality and good will. But the remarkable thing here is how quickly the crew changes its mind about the character of the Mariner's deed. Their evaluation (in the space of one **stanza** in the poem) changes from condemnation of the Mariner to praise of him: "Then all averred, I had killed the bird / That brought the fog and mist. / 'Twas right, said they, such birds to slay, / That bring the fog and mist." Their change of heart binds them in guilt with the Mariner. The gloss puts it that they "make themselves accomplices in the crime."

It is some time before it becomes clear that the killing of the Albatross is an offense against nature and that the guilty ones must suffer the punishment that the offended universe feels. The progress of the voyage into the Pacific is not interrupted by natural forces. One could almost get the impression in **stanza** five that the whole thing had been forgotten: "The fair breeze blew, the white foam flew, / The furrow followed free...." But suddenly, with the same shocking abruptness with which the Mariner let fly the killing shaft at the Albatross, the wind dies: the ship is stilled! The process of punishment has begun.

This is the place in the poem of those three **stanzas** that every school child memorizes, **stanzas** seven, eight, and nine.

All in a hot and copper sky, The bloody Sun, at noon, Right up above the mast did stand, No bigger than the Moon

Day after day, day after day, We stuck, nor breath nor motion; As idle as a painted ship Upon a painted ocean.

Water, water, everywhere, And all the boards did shrink; Water, water, everywhere, Nor any drop to drink.

Notice the words that emphasize the position of the sun at noon at the Equator: hot, copper, bloody, and "No bigger than the Moon." In "Christabel" the "lovely lady" of the poem meets the witch Geraldine under a moon that is "both small and dull." Coleridge's use of natural objects and atmosphere is usually quite telling. The world about the ship is described in **stanza** nine as a world in decay, "The very deep did rot. . . ." This is the world the ship is becalmed in, a world dead of its usual natural beauties. The creatures of the sea are "slimy things." The only beautiful distraction from the rotting world is the death-fires that dance at night and the water that burns "green, and blue and white." Again an ambiguity: the beauty of the deadly. We think again of Geraldine.

Stanza twelve, telling as it does of a Spirit that plagues the ship, recalls the preface to the poem from T. Burnet about the invisible beings that live in the universe. The gloss summarizes the matter: "A Spirit had followed them; one of the invisible inhabitants of this planet, neither departed souls nor angels; concerning whom the learned Jew, Josephus, and the Platonic Constantinopolitan, Michael Psellus, may be consulted. They are very numerous, and there is no climate or element without one or more."

One of the most savagely painful parts of the punishment that the crew undergoes is thirst: "And every tongue, through utter drought, / Was withered at the root; / We could not speak, nor more than if / We had been choked with soot."

By the time one comes to the end of Part II, one can no longer be unaware of the abrupt transitions that are made in the progress of the poem, both in narration and in dialogue. At the end of Part II we are told with the same suddenness that characterized the account of the Mariner's murder of the Albatross at the end of Part I that the dead Albatross is hung by the crew around the Mariner's neck; they wish to put all of their guilt on him - hardly atypical behavior for mortals.

Comment

The sea journey on which the ancient Mariner takes the Wedding-Guest by means of this gripping, even imprisoning, power of storytelling shows Coleridge using one of the most time-tested techniques in literature. Mention was made before of Melville's sea journey in *Moby Dick*. The reader of "The Ancient Mariner" would find interesting comparisons in the use of the same literary technique in such additional works as Homer's *Odyssey*, Virgil's *Aeneid*, Defoe's *Robinson Crusoe*. But, somehow, land travel does not, for all its appeal and charm, touch the depths of our own mysterious selves the way sea travel does. Chaucer's Canterbury pilgrimage is delightful, but it does not gather us on a flood of deep, mysteriously deep, emotional significance and carry us along to the dim edges of our being, where dream and waking consciousness are no longer distinguishable, where we meet with sights and sounds that may be a million years old, where dark and light, sun and ice blend into legion designs, and separate again into legion others. Only tales of the sea can do that. Voyages more than travels on land have a kind of cosmic significance - they take us for reasons that we do not really understand to shores beyond the limits of man's mortal, landlocked self. The rolling contours of the sea seem to give us a welcomed liberation from the rigid lines and angles of the world where reality makes us live.

The crew's relations with the Mariner move again with nearly the degree of caprice that unfolds in other parts of the poem. The crew first defends the Mariner's deed, then condemns, but the significant difference is that they do defend and condemn on the basis of the degree of fortune or misfortune that befalls the ship. Perhaps this fact cannot be talked about as caprice, but the extent of their commitment to the Mariner, whether for his right or his wrong, is so thin as to have the character of caprice. If the crew is a collection of mankind, how dismal a comment the act of shipmate to shipmate is on the capacity of man for faithful relationship.

The interaction of the poet with nature, even of man in general with nature, was a question with which Coleridge (and Wordsworth) struggled, but never really answered. The essence of the matter is the question of whether nature, its objects and forces, give man life, or whether nature can only live because man animates it through projecting into it his dynamic, enlivening power of imagination. Coleridge, if one takes his poetry as a whole, would probably have it both ways, Wordsworth probably also. In considering the way nature is seen after the becalming of the ship, a comment that Coleridge made in one of his notebooks about the interrelationships of man with nature can be easily thought of : "In looking at objects of Nature I seem rather to be seeking, as it were asking, for, a symbolical language, for something within me that already and for ever exists, than observing anything new." The quality and quantity of man's relationship with nature is never really settled in "The Ancient Mariner" either.

The Sun stands directly above the ship at the time of the calm. There are eleven references to the Sun throughout the poem. It might be considered as associated in Coleridge's mind with that side of God's action that one would call judgment. There are fourteen references to the Moon in the poem. Are there consistent associations with the Sun and the Moon throughout the poem? If the Sun is associated in Part II with the judging and punishing side of God's nature, it would seem a logical possibility that the Moon could be associated with His Grace and forgiveness. There is certainly no denying that the poem is full of theological references in the stricter sense of the theology of the Judeo-Christian tradition; but it has also religious elements that go much beyond the formally theological.

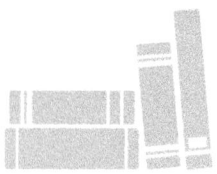

THE RIME OF THE ANCIENT MARINER

TEXTUAL ANALYSIS

PART III

The main event of this part of the poem is the appearance of the skeleton ship. On board the ship are the figures of Death and Life-in-Death. The Spectre-Woman is called "The Night-mare Life-In-Death." Death is the woman's mate. The ship-mates of the Mariner are claimed by Death; Life-in-Death takes the Mariner as her own. Casting dice is the means used by Death and Life-in-Death to determine the destiny of all the men on board.

The first **stanza** tells of the passing of a weary time; the word weary is used four times in one **stanza**, but weary may not communicate to us at first the scorching agony: "Each throat / Was parched, and glazed each eye." At the end of this first **stanza**, the Mariner's weary eye catches a faint object.

The object compared to mist in **stanzas** two and three, appears at first as no more than a speck. As it comes nearer it gives the impression to the Mariner's eye of moving so restlessly (**stanza** three) that it might be dodging a water-sprite (one of Coleridge's superbly subtle imaginative images): "As if it dodged a water-sprite, / It plunged and tacked and veered."

Stanza four (the Mariner now having pointed out the ship to his fellow sailors) reports the state of their suffering in the terms of the awful psychological experience of wanting to speak but not being able to. Again the nightmare universe of the poem! The seeing of the ship and not being able to utter any sound of joy or dread, of welcome or rejection, has the horror of paralysis in a dream, being shut up, imprisoned by one's own mind, struggling to speak and wake up but remaining closed within one's own smothering isolation: "With throats unslaked, with black lips baked, / We could nor laugh nor wail, / Through utter drought all dumb we stood!" The skeleton ship comes nearer, and the Mariner remembers the blood in his veins. He bites his arm in order to be able to hail the ship. His mates thank him in surprise and repeat the act for themselves. The reader may remember certain similarly gruesome touches in the Gothic novel, but Coleridge uses such situations of horror with restraint and artistic balance. But the "flash of joy," as the gloss describes the crew's reaction to the ship, is soon burned out. There is the horror - struck realization that a ship cannot move on this windless sea without being propelled by some supernatural power, probably more destroying than saving, perhaps the first response of any crew to the supernatural.

Stanza seven gives the time as the end of the day. The Sun falls down the sky from the Mariner's vantage point and has nearly reached the top of the wave. At this time the skeleton ship imposes itself within the Mariner's line of sight by moving between the sun and the ship. The specter-bark itself is being presented in close association with the Sun. Within twelve lines beginning at line four in **stanza** seven, the Sun is named five times: "Rested the broad bright Sun," "Betwixt us and the Sun," "And straight the Sun was flecked with bars," "Are those her sails that glance in the Sun," "Are those her ribs through which the Sun." **Stanza** eight, which contains a prayer to the Virgin Mary for grace, has the Sun "As if through a dungeon-grate he peered / With broad and burning face." The **simile** certainly does not stress a soft light of kindness or of merciful care. This is a glaring Sun, fixedly burning upon his subjects. Notice that the prayer is of the nature of an interjection in the midst of the account of the Sun's intensity.

The Mariner asks questions of identification about the mysterious ship in **stanzas** nine and ten. Coleridge's characteristic sensitivity to light and cloud comes through in his comparison of the ribs of the ship to the bars of cloud over the Sun. Who sails this ship? This question ends **stanza** ten: "And is that Woman all her crew? / Is that a Death?: and are there two? / Is Death that woman's mate?" The answer comes in the following **stanza** in a description of the woman, "The Night-mare Life-In-Death." She is a kind of harlot figure:

Her lips were red, her looks were free, Her locks were yellow as gold: Her skin was as white as leprosy, The Night-mare Life-In-Death was she Who thicks man's blood with cold.

In the following **stanza** she whistles thrice, declaring herself to be the winner in the game of chance with her partner. The Mariner hears his fate as the specter-bark comes along side.

Almost immediately it is night; **stanza** thirteen tells of the setting of the Sun, the nearly aggressive coming of night ("the stars rush out") and the disappearance, again with great speed, of the skeleton ship. The gloss reminds us that we are "within the courts of the Sun." No dim, visionary light here, as in the *Conversation Poems*. This is the arena of absolute meeting with all the elemental forces of the universe. It is either scorching light or heavy dark.

Stanza fourteen moves the Mariner and his doomed crew into darkness with only pin points of light piercing the gloom. Thick night, dim stars, one lamp on the ship, the face of the steersman reflecting the lamp, and then "The horned Moon, with one bright star / Within the nether tip." If the crime that the ancient Mariner committed brought on the Sun, we might expect the reverse with the Moon, that at the rising of the Moon some act of goodness, some action or event favorable to the Mariner and the crew would happen. We will find it so in the next part, but here in the remaining three stanzas, not so. Each one of the two-hundred men under the newly risen Moon curses the Mariner and falls down dead. To their separate unknown destinies the souls of the men go with the sound (and speed) of the Mariner's cross-bow. He is left alone, absolutely alone, having only in his ears the "heavy thump" with which the souls left their bodies behind.

Comment

One of the fiercest elements of terror in the meeting of the Mariner and his crew with the skeleton ship is that a game of chance is used to determine their judgment. It is difficult not to associate this with the caprice of other incidents in the poem. Indeed, with what has happened only to the end of Part III, it is easy to see that the capricious is the very heart of the poem. The dice with which those two awful forms on the specter-bark cast the doom of the ship are a little too much like loaded dice. This whole **episode** calls into question the poem as a work that simply carries out the remorseless action of crime and punishment. There is not only the question of whether the punishment is in proportion to the crime. There is the further question of whether this is the way in which punishment is determined in an orderly universe. The events of the part of the poem we have just read raise some serious questions about making "The Ancient Mariner" into the dramatization of some established philosophical system or some systematically structured theological interpretation of man's relationship with God and the universe. How much of a consistent, logical interpretation can we really make of this series of events, whatever the system of thought happens to be? The events of Part III have certainly more of the character of a nightmare universe than the character of a universe where there is really the harmony of a God who is divinely in his creation and divinely above it, inspiring it from within and beneficently guiding it with sovereign fatherhood from without. Is God's retribution so weirdly and haphazardly administered? Theological assumptions or statements throughout Coleridge's poetry are anything but consistent, anything but consistent even within individual poems. Sometimes as in "The Eolian Harp": he even tries to pass off magic for philosophy and then call the whole package humble Christian Faith. The Christian concepts of sin, judgment and redemption, even with a reading of the Old Testament through Christian eyes, find little substantial articulation in the events of "The Ancient Mariner." The haphazard developments of Part III will hardly support such a reading.

Looking forward to later parts of the poem, the reader should certainly keep the third part in mind, especially when he comes to what is generally called the "moral" of the poem: "He prayeth best who loveth best / All things both great and small; / For the dear God who loveth us, / He made and loveth all." It is almost characteristic of Coleridge to try, as with poems he was not satisfied with, to sweep chaotic dust under an apologetic rug. There is almost a separate **genre** in Coleridge's work of "apologetic prefaces." We have grown suspicious of such "explanations" as the one Coleridge gave of the man from Porlock who interrupted the recollection of the dream that is "Kubla Khan."

How guilty are the crew? Do they deserve the judgment to death that they receive? It is true that they make themselves accomplices to the Mariner's crime by agreeing with the deed. But, they are the usual kinds of mortals that one meets in the classroom, fraternity house, supermarket, jury. They are just fickle persons, like most persons. But the preciousness of their life, however sorry they may be as poor, shabby creatures, is insulted by the formidable forces of whim on the ghost ship, dishing out destiny according to the way the dice roll. Life-in-Death and Death could only have contempt for life. The ruthless arbitrariness of the pronouncement, and the whistle of victory are stunning, staggering! If a person had to live in this kind of universe, he might not be brave enough to settle for opium - a pistol ball would work all too slowly.

Studies have been written on the way in which the poem is really a projection of Coleridge's own fearful, guilt-ridden internal world. Perhaps the personal element can never really be eliminated from the production of any work of art, even of any criticism of art. But it is the vexing question of how far to go in order to get everything out of a poem that a poet put into it without putting the reader's own attitudes - and neuroses - into the poem and consequently making it say things that are not really part of its world and experience. However, it does not seem too far to go, particularly because of the character of other poems Coleridge wrote, to say that the unpredictable, uncontrollable universe in which he found himself too often was out of keeping with the harmonious universe he wanted to discover and proclaim. The conflict keeps creeping into the poetry; with "The Ancient Mariner" it stalks in. Of course, the most profound reaches of the cleavage are always within, for it is ultimately there that any universe exists, whatever its character and behavior.

The **epitaph** that Coleridge wrote for himself in 1833 may add one last consideration to the question of biographical criticism of this part of the poem: the passer-by is asked to "lift one thought in prayer for S. T. C. / That He, who many a year with toilsome breath /Found Death in Life, may here find Life in Death."

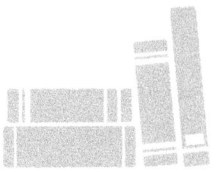

THE RIME OF THE ANCIENT MARINER

TEXTUAL ANALYSIS

PART IV

....

This might be called the central part of the poem; it is the turning point in the whole action of the drama. This is not to say, of course, that in this part the Mariner is freed from the suffering of his penance, for he remains subject to that to the end of the poem, and beyond. But, in Part IV the Mariner experiences a conversion, and the term conversion in the theological sense does not seem out of place considering the deeply religious nature of the experience the Mariner has when he blesses the watersnakes unaware.

The Wedding-Guest renews his protest of the Mariner's hold over him in the first two **stanzas** of Part IV. The focus of his objection in these two opening **stanzas** is that he fears the Mariner to be a Spirit:

'I fear thee, ancient Mariner! I fear thy skinny hand! And thou art long, and lank, and brown, As is the ribbed sea-sand. I fear thee and thy glittering eye, And thy skinny hand, so brown.' -

Coleridge uses the words long and lank as a part of his description of the Mariner in **stanza** one. The same words appear in a description of the dell in "This Lime-Tree Bower my Prison," a poem also from the year 1797. The words long and lank in "Lime-Tree Bower" are intended to help create a feeling about the dell as being fearsome, awesome. The same effect is intended here about the Mariner. Coleridge said that Wordsworth contributed the lines in which the words long and lank appear in "The Ancient Mariner," lines three and four of **stanza** one.

The Mariner assures the Wedding-Guest in the last of **stanza** two that he need not fear him as a ghost: "Fear not, fear not, thou Wedding-Guest! / This body dropt not down." The gloss has it, ". . . the ancient Mariner assureth him of his bodily life. . . ." In all of the incidents of the Wedding - Guest's protests in the poem, mention is made of the Mariner's glittering eye.

Stanzas three through eleven inclusive may be read as the account of the utter isolation of the Mariner, the first principal stage of his penance, the initiation into the agonizing loneliness that will afflict him from time to time throughout his life. He begins to tell of this absolute separation from God and man in **stanza** three; this stanza is the most concentrated statement of the Mariner's isolation:

Alone, alone, all, all alone, Alone on a wide wide sea! And never a saint took pity on My soul in agony.

The isolation is agony, and in his future life the only way in which he can relieve the agony is to tell the story of his experience. **Stanza** three anticipates the fuller explanation of the penance that will come in Part VII. In **stanza** fifteen and sixteen of Part VII, Coleridge will use the word agony again for the state of isolation of the Mariner that we first learn of here in Part IV.

Stanza four reflects the extent of the Mariner's hatred of himself: as a means of self-punishment he looks upon the men who lie dead around him and speaks of their being "so beautiful"; he puts their beauty as human selves as a whip into the hand of his own sense of guilt, that is, he lashes himself with the fact of what they were. There is the further connection in this **stanza** made between the beauty of the dead men and the ugliness of his own life as it is bound up with the ugliness of the "thousand thousand slimy things" that live on around him. The **stanza** bespeaks a king of metaphysical rebellion: why should the Mariner, feeling the deep sense of revulsion that he does toward himself, live on, and why should the hideous creatures of the sea live on when all the human creatures around him are dead? As with most questions of **metaphysical** rebellion no answer is forthcoming. (Compare William Blake's "The Tiger.") The Mariner's rebellion against the action of the universe is spelled out in the gloss to **stanzas** four and five: "He despiseth the creatures of the calm, / And envieth that they should live and so many lie dead."

Stanza five continues to relate the Mariner's disgust at his surroundings. Is it that his own condemnation of himself causes him to see things external to himself as disgusting?

I looked upon the rotting sea, And drew my eyes away; I looked upon the rotting deck, And there the dead men lay.

Is the sea a "rotting sea" because he in his soul is a rotting man? Or is the world around him actually in its own right, apart from the way he sees it, a rotting world because it is in a deep sympathetic relationship with his actions, because there is "one Life within us and abroad," because over all of the "organic Harps [of animated nature] diversely fram'd ... sweeps / Plastic and vast, one intellectual breeze, / At once the Soul of each, and God of all?"

Questions of extreme **metaphysical** import continue to be asked in stanza six, although it may be more accurate, given the Christian character of the poem, to speak of the questions as theological rather than just metaphysical. The report the Mariner gives in **stanza** six of his inability to pray raises the whole problem of the freedom of the human will. How much ability does man have within himself to find his own salvation? The Mariner tries to pray for help, but before he can utter his prayer, he finds himself uttering evil:

I looked to heaven, and tried to pray; But or ever a prayer had gusht, A wicked whisper came, and made My heart as dry as dust.

If the Mariner drew his eyes away from the rotting sea in **stanza** five, in **stanza** seven he draws his eyes away from his own rotting self. He has just in **stanza** six recognized his own depravity (the familiar Calvinistic term does not seem out of place); he has just had the crushing realization that he is "not unlucky but evil," to use W. H. Auden's words of man's condition; he has had the experience Paul talks about in his Letter to the Romans: "The good which I want to do, I fail to do; but what I do is the wrong which is against my will. . . ." In **stanza** seven, then, he closes his eyes to his own self and to his own condition:

I closed my lids, and kept them close, And the balls like pulses beat; For the sky and the sea, and the sea and the sky Lay like a load on my weary eye, And the dead were at my feet.

For the time of seven days the curse of the dead shipmates is fixed on the Mariner. **Stanzas** eight and nine tell that 1) the bodies of the sailors did not decay, 2) that the curse in the sailors' eyes for the Mariner is fixed horribly on him, so horribly that he would wish to die, and 3) that although he wishes to die he cannot.

Taking the whole of Part IV as a turning point in the drama of the Mariner's "crime and punishment," though such a phrase can all too superficially pass over so many of the serious elements in the poem, the action can be more exactly specified by pointing to **stanza** ten as the beginning of the Mariner's redemption. No student of the poem should miss how light and color figure into this process of redemption. Exacting attention should be placed on the effects of the Moon, stars, water, and, of course, on the central spectacle in the whole phantasmagoria of light and color, the creatures of the ocean, designated now, as it is so absolutely necessary to recognize, not as "slimy things," but rather in the simple objective terms' "water-snakes." Something has already begun to happen in the way the Mariner sees the phenomena around him - perhaps because of the light of the Moon. It may be entirely right to say that the Mariner's redemption begins to "move" when the Moon begins moving up the sky. This **stanza** tells of the Mariner's first awareness of the beauty of natural phenomena after his killing of the Albatross. He has commented on it before, for example in the appearance of the Sun in Part II, but this is the beginning of any real involvement in the beauty of nature after his crime.

The Mariner's ejaculation of praise for the creatures of the deep - **stanza** fourteen - follows immediately upon the description of the beauty of the sky and sea. For four stanzas, beginning with stanza ten, the Mariner describes the beauty of what he saw under the Moon: let the reader observe the use of light and color: the Moon goes up the sky with stars following; the light of the Moon is compared to frost; there is water of an awe-inspiring red (this is not only a "lifeless ocean" as in "Kubla Khan," but it is a "charmed" one as well); the water-snakes that the Mariner sees "Beyond the shadow of the ship" move "in tracks of shining white" (flashing with golden fire), and drop about them flakes of white light when they rise above the surface of the water; besides, the snakes are clothed in the colors of "Blue, glossy green, and velvet black." The whole encounter has the magical about it, but, Coleridge in the gloss talks about what he sees in religious terms: "By the light of the Moon he beholdeth God's creatures of the great calm."

Probably the most important lines in the two **stanzas** that tell at the end of Part IV of the Mariner's redemption are the third and fourth lines in **stanza** fourteen: "A spring of love gushed from my heart, / And I blessed them unaware. . . ." Throughout the poem runs the **theme** of the uncontrollable: there has been the Mariner's crime of killing the Albatross for reasons that he does not express and does not know; there has been the administration of punishment by Life-In-Death and Death while the Mariner watches helplessly and dumbfounded. Now, for reasons that are unexplained and unknown to the Mariner, he finds that the very creatures he has called "a thousand thousand slimy things," he now can speak of as "happy living things," as things so beautiful that they cannot be described. Line five in **stanza** fourteen has the only explanation that the Mariner can give: "Sure my kind saint took pity on me. . . ." This is the same as saying that his conversion of heart and his redemption (though perhaps they should be stated the other way around) are given by grace, not in any way earned by goodness of thought or deed on his part; his salvation, that is, comes from outside himself. The last **stanza** in this part tells the result of his redemption, the result of his blessing the creatures of the deep: When he blesses them unaware he becomes able to pray, and at that moment the Albatross falls off from around his neck:

The self-same moment I could pray; And from my neck so free The Albatross fell off, and sank Like lead into the sea.

This is the beginning (see the gloss to the last **stanza**) of the breaking of the drought and the calm.

Comment

One of the great defects of "The Ancient Mariner" that Wordsworth named was that the Mariner "has no distinct character, either in his profession of Mariner, or as a human being who having been long under the control of supernatural impressions might be supposed himself to partake of something supernatural: that he does not act, but is continually acted upon. . . ." Irving Babbitt in more recent times commented that other than his killing of the Albatross, the Mariner does not really engage in any action in the poem, that he could not be called an agent. But for all the absence of what we and others might call human qualities or characteristics in the Mariner, he has much of the quality of a poet. The Mariner tells of a fantastic experience, an experience that sounds so supernatural to the Wedding-Guest that he keeps fearing the Mariner, even to the point here in Part IV of thinking him a Spirit.

The characteristic of the Mariner that is mentioned most frequently in the poem is his bright, glittering eye. This is not at all surprising considering how often in Coleridge's poetry we have particular power attributed to the eye. The parallel that comes most immediately to mind is, of course, the young poet in "Kubla Khan" with flashing eyes and floating hair, who would build a pleasure dome in air if he could only recall the music of the Abyssinian maid whom he once saw in a vision. There is in Coleridge's "Christabel" also a provocative number of incidents that involve the power of the eye. As noted above in the analysis of <u>Part IV</u>, whenever the Wedding - Guest makes objection to the Mariner's hold over him, there is in the stanza or **stanzas** of protest the naming of the bright, glittering eye of the Mariner. Besides the power of the Mariner's eye, he is exiled from the human community as a result of the strange things he has seen, and he brings fear to those who hear of his mysterious adventures. And, of course, he is gifted with "strange power of speech."

The Moon and moonlight have a special place in Coleridge's poems; they are used in almost numberless poetic connections. One remembers Coleridge's "**Sonnet** on the Autumnal Moon," where the name given the Moon is "Mother of wildly-working visions," and "Songs of the Pixies," where the Moon is "Mother of wildly-working dreams. "Of course, "Christabel" is full of moonlight, and the "deep romantic chasm" in "Kubla Khan" has a setting "beneath a waning moon." There has been much discussion of the fact that the Mariner's salvation begins when the Moon softly rises and bemocks "the sultry main." In one of the most famous essays written on "The Ancient Mariner," Robert Penn Warren says that all the bad things happen in the poem when the Sun is dominant and that all the good things happen under the influence of the Moon. George Herbert Clarke in an article on symbols in the poem writes of the Sun as a symbol of the God of Law and the Moon as the symbol of the God of Love. Mr. Clarke points out the striking contrast that comes in Part IV when the Mariner stands in the midst of a rotting ocean, a rotting deck, two - hundred dead men, with the curse in the eyes of the dead men fixed on him, and sees the Moon rising softly. He associates this softly-rising Moon with the gentleness of God's love and mercy. But, there is in Part III, stanza fourteen, the association of the Moon with the death of the crew, when they curse the Mariner and fall down without sigh or groan. That Moon was a "horned Moon, with one bright star / Within the nether tip." Between the "star - dogged Moon" under which the sailors die and the rising Moon under which the Mariner finds beauty in the world, there is perhaps an all-important difference in phase and aspect. Coleridge's manuscript note may help to clarify the matter: "It is a common superstition among sailors, 'that something evil is about to happen, whenever a star dogs the Moon.' "Disaster occurs under a Moon that has a star within the horns, whereas redemption occurs when there is with the Moon "a star or two beside."

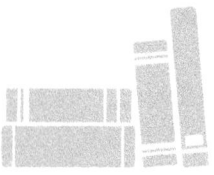

THE RIME OF THE ANCIENT MARINER

TEXTUAL ANALYSIS

PART V

The breaking of the spell that has bound the Mariner began with the Albatross falling of his neck and into the sea. Now in Part V rain and wind, requisites off life for man and ship, return, though strangely it is not the wind that propels the ship. Life seems to return also to the dead crew, but as the Mariner clarifies to the frightened Wedding-Guest, the souls of the men have not returned to their bodies, rather the men have become animated "by a blessed troop of angelic spirits, send down by the invocation of the guardian saint." The ship is propelled as far as the Equator by "The lonesome Spirit from the south pole." At noon the ship stops, for upon reaching the Equator the Polar Spirit stops propelling it. But after a minute of calm, the ship lunges forward again, this time under angelic power, and with such speed that the Mariner swoons. When he awakes he hears his "long and heavy" penance discussed by two voices;

the two voices he overhears belong to "The Polar Spirit's fellow-daemons, the invisible inhabitants of the element."

Part V is a very confusing part of the poem. It is not at all easy to follow the action. We are not told anything at all with regard to the ship's return voyage to England around the Cape of Good Hope. Even a person who knows the poem very well may stumble in an explanation about the movements of the ship in this part of the poem. This is not to say that the overall quality of "The Ancient Mariner" is actually marred by what happens and is not fully explained in Part V. On the contrary, paucity of detail may serve to heighten the supernatural quality of the action. However, calling attention to some facts that do not get a particularly explicit presentation in the poem may assist the reader's comprehension of Part V: 1) the Polar Spirit that drives the ship to the Equator does so under the direction of the angelic spirits; 2) the Voices that discuss the Mariner's penance are not angelic spirits, but rather they are fellow-daemons to the Polar Spirit; 3) there is a kind of bargain made between the Polar Spirit and the troop of angelic spirits after which the mariner's penance is exacted; 4) the Polar Spirit takes leave of the ship when it reaches the Line.

Stanza one is in praise of sleep and of the Virgin Mary; the Mariner gives credit and praise to Mary for sending "the gentle sleep from Heaven" with which he is blessed immediately after the Albatross falls from him into the sea. Notice the use of the word gentle in this first **stanza**, and be particularly mindful of the effect of the verb slid in the lines, "She sent the gentle sleep from Heaven, / That slid into my soul." It is an excellent choice of word for impressing on the reader's feelings the gentleness of the sleep that the Mariner felt. These early **stanzas** in Part V emphasize the extreme drought that had punished the Mariner, through the very sharp contrast with his present state of refreshment under a cooling, soaking rain.

Stanza two tells of the Mariner's dream that precedes and predicts the rain. His dream before the rain is that the buckets on the deck of the ship "That had so long remained, / . . . were filled with dew. . . ." The dream is a wonderful demonstration of the symbol-making power of man. A drought - stricken man, a painfully thirsty man, would of course dream of empty buckets - empty man, empty buckets! The parallel is unquestionable; we could hardly doubt that Coleridge had actually had such a dream. In **stanza** two the rain follows immediately upon the dream. As the buckets were filled with curative dew in the Mariner's dream, so is the Mariner's body filled with the curative rain. Anyone who has been caught and soaked in a heavy rain will feel stanza three; observe Coleridge's use of d sounds in this stanza:

My lips were wet, my throat was cold, My garments all were dank Sure I had drunken in my dreams, And still my body drank.

The effect of the rain falling on this parched man is to make his body seem not a body anymore. The weariness of his condition has been so washed away in the rain that he thinks himself no longer alive as a human: "I was so light-almost / I thought that I had died in sleep, / And was a blessed ghost." But, he thinks of "blessed ghost" as **metaphor** for his present glad relief from suffering because he has still the vivid memory of wanting so much in the midst of his agony to be relieved of weary life altogether.

One of the most difficult aspects of the interpretation of Part V is the action of the wind. **Stanza** five tells of the Mariner's hearing "a roaring wind," but strangely it does not come near.

This becomes particularly confusing when the reader reaches **stanza** seven, for there the Mariner speaks of "the coming wind." But, the wind does not come, as the first line of stanza nine clarifies: "The loud wind never reached the ship...." There is the emphasis in **stanzas** five, six, seven, and nine on the loud, even the roaring kind of wind that this is. But still it does not come near the ship; the sails of the ship shake but only with the sound of the wind.

And soon I heard a roaring wind: It did not come anear; But with its sound it shook the sails, That were so thin and sear.

The gloss to **stanza** five stresses the "commotions in the sky and the element." At least one way to think of this event is to take the wind that one hears but does not feel as an anticipation, as a hope for a better condition in life than one presently knows, that is, the wind could be interpreted as a new life that announces itself from a distance, and, therefore, from the future.

The strange panorama of sights continues in **stanza** six with the upper air bursting into life, with "a hundred fire-flags sheen," with wan stars dancing between.

Line three of **stanza** seven identifies the source of the rain as "one black cloud." It seems not accidental, given the other presences and influences of the Moon in the poem, that the storm occurs within the abiding influence of the Moon; **stanzas** seven and eight tell that during the storm the Moon is at the edge of that "one black cloud." Further evidence of the regenerating influence of the Moon can be found in **stanza** nine: here the Mariner tells of the beginning of the reanimation of the dead men by the angelic spirits. The first evidence of their resuscitation is a groan that the dead men give "Beneath the lightning and the Moon...."

The strangeness of what the Mariner sees when the dead men stir into life finds expression in **stanza** ten. He tells that the spectacle of the dead coming back to life would have been strange even if it had occurred in a dream. When they rise from their lifeless state, they neither speak nor move their eyes.

Stanza eleven reiterates that the ship moved on although there was no wind present. Each member of the crew goes to his regular post and begins to do his accustomed work. But, the Mariner is careful to specify that the men are not really men; they are only corpses able to carry out the working of the ship's apparatus because they are vivified and energized by the angelic spirits that have entered into their bodies. The last lines in **stanza** eleven and the incident of the Mariner's meeting the body of his nephew in stanza twelve make this fact evident. The limbs of the crew are lifeless, and the Mariner's nephew is only a body:

The mariners all 'gan work the ropes, Where they were wont to do; They raised their limbs like lifeless tools - We were a ghastly crew.

The body of my brother's son Stood by me, knee to knee: The body and I pulled at one rope, But he said nought to me.

Stanza thirteen of Part V renews the Wedding-Guest's apprehensive protest. The Mariner seeks to calm him with the assurance that the souls of the dead crew did not return to their corpses, but rather that the bodies became reanimated by angelic spirits.

The following four stanzas, fourteen, fifteen, sixteen and seventeen, introduce the auditory parallel to the tactile experience of the refreshing, restoring rain. At dawn (**stanza** fourteen) the crew gathers round the mast to sing: "Sweet sounds rose slowly through their mouths, / And from their bodies passed." The music is a celebration of the Mariner's recovery of life. Stanza fifteen tells how the music that comes from the crew reverberates in the heavens. There is variety of tone in the music:

Slowly the sounds came back again, Now mixed, now one by one. . . .

And now 'twas like all instruments, Now like a lonely flute; And now it is an angel's song, That makes the heavens be mute.

In the midst of the music that the Mariner hears from the mouths of the men, he finds himself sensitive to the song of the skylark and to "all other little birds that are. . . ." There has been an upward movement in the Mariner's renewed awareness of the beauty of creation. First, he saw in a new way the beauty of the creatures of the deep; now he hears in a new way the beauty of the creatures of the sky. His regenerated sensitivity to his surroundings is evident also in that he hears the sounds of the sails - all this following the music of the spirits - as:

A pleasant noise till noon, A noise like of a hidden brook In the leafy month of June, That to the sleeping woods all night Singeth a quiet tune. (**stanza** eighteen)

The Mariner's experiences to this point in Part V have all been of such a redeeming and consequently hopeful kind that he can think of the sound of the sails in the terms of quiet and sleep.

We may read **stanza** nineteen as the end of this major section of Part V, for the remaining **stanzas** take on a different cast. Stanza nineteen tells of quiet sailing (in harmony with the Mariner's state of mind and soul at this time) without any wind: "Slowly and smoothly went the ship, / Moved onward from beneath."

At **stanza** twenty the progress of the ship is stopped, for the Polar Spirit takes his leave:

Under the keel nine fathom deep, From the land of mist and snow, The spirit slid: and it was he That made the ship to go.

Anyone following Coleridge's use of the Sun through the poem as a possibly consistent symbol will observe that the Sun is again right above the mast when the ship halts at the Line. **Stanza** twenty-one has it that the Sun "Had fixed [the ship] to the ocean. . . ." But the effort to discover a consonant use of the Sun as symbol throughout the poem is complicated by the fact that as the ship stopped under the Sun, it starts again under the Sun. It is not so easy here in **stanzas** twenty, twenty-one, and twenty-two to arrive at a definite conclusion that what is happening under the influence of the Sun is bad. In only a minute after the Polar Spirit has left off propelling the ship, (**stanza** twenty-one), the ship begins to stir again, and then (**stanza** twenty-two) the ship bounds forward suddenly, "like a pawing horse let go. . . ."

The sudden lunging forward of the ship throws the Mariner down into a swoon, for the motion, which brings the blood rushing into his head, is more than is humanly bearable (**stanza** twenty-two). He remains for an undetermined time in the swoon (**stanza** twenty-three), but when he awakes he hears a conversation between "Two voices in the air," two of the fellow-daemons of the Polar Spirit. Their exchange will continue into Part VI. The first thing that the Mariner can discern in what they say is that he is identified as the villain who killed the Albatross.

'Is it he? quoth one, 'Is this the man? By him who died on cross, With his cruel bow he laid full low The harmless Albatross.'

There may be more intended in the vow than the customary appeal to the divine for authority; perhaps the intent is to associate the harmless Christ with the harmless Albatross. In the discussion that goes on between the two daemons, there is the clarification that the Polar Spirit loved the Albatross (**stanza** twenty-five) and that, as the gloss has it, "penance long and heavy for the ancient Mariner hath been accorded to the Polar Spirit...." The Spirit from the south pole, who has worked under the directions of the angelic spirits, has now returned to "the land of mist and snow." Part V ends on the heavy note, "The man hath penance done, / And penance more will do."

Comment

The relationships that exist in the poem between the various kinds of spiritual beings are not easily settled. As suggested above, the angelic spirits that come in a troop to bring the dead crew into such a state of animation that they can work the ship, these angelic spirits have sovereign power over the daemons of the elements, and they take the command of the ship away from these daemons. Consequently, the Polar Spirit does his work under the power and direction of the angelic spirits. It is, of course, the angelic spirits that direct the eventual return of the ship to its home harbor, although there is the presence of the wind during the voyage. The angelic spirits also exercise a beneficent influence over the Polar Spirit, for although he has come on a mission of revenge, he is subdued into the service of the ship. This is not to say, of course, that the Polar Spirit at this time gives up his intent for vengeance. There is in the Polar Spirit's vengeance the suggestion (or the revelation) of a bond of relationship that exists between him and the Albatross, and there is consequently the suggestion that the Albatross is a source of power for the direction of the processes of nature.

The buckets of which the Mariner dreams are described with the word silly (**stanza** two). We may profitably recall something of the etymology of the word. The Old English saelig had the meaning, as Professor Walter W. Skeat points out, of "happy, lucky, blessed, innocent." Coleridge would have been aware of these meanings. The important thing for us to see is that the very buckets on the deck participate in the Mariner's experience of redemption. In the blessed sleep that follows on his being relieved of the burden of the Albatross around his neck, the grace of his redemption extends even to the inanimate objects around him; he dreams of the objects most closely associated with water, the element that his penance has so far deprived him of. In one sense the blessing of the "silly buckets on the deck" repeats with inanimate objects the blessing that he gave unaware to the water-snakes of the deep.

The association of the Mariner's condemnation with drought and his redemption with rain is not at all surprising, considering how many of Coleridge's poems have the drought/fertility contrast, particularly with regard to settings for inspirational experiences. This is not to ignore the more traditional association of water and life in literature generally.

The action of the wind in this part of the poem can be perplexing. Two facts are obvious: 1) the movement of the wind is certainly mysterious, and 2) the wind is certainly one of the most important elements in the goings-on in Part V. The one most confusing characteristic of the wind here, of course, is that it blows loudly but does not either touch the Mariner or influence the ship, except that the sound of it shakes the sails.

The Mariner cannot think of it as inspirational because it does not blow across him, and he cannot think of it as a beneficial force in nature that drives the ship toward its destination. The gloss does not help very much, for we are only told that the Mariner "heareth sounds and seeth strange sights and commotions in the sky and the element."

There is the possible means of interpretation of turning to the "archetypes," the established character and function of the wind in legend and literature. Besides the numerous incidents of poets using the wind as a creative force, one recalls the presence of wind as the expression of the Spirit of God in any number of places in Biblical literature: there is the vision of Ezekiel, there is the spirit that bloweth where it listeth in the Fourth Gospel, there is in the Book of Acts the Holy Spirit descending with the sound of a mighty wind. But we are not confined for help in interpretation to traditional associations. There are a number of suggestions that can come from Coleridge himself. One thinks most immediately of the plea, even the prayer, that the poet makes to the wind in "Dejection: An Ode" that it will come and stir his defunct imagination to life:

And oh! that even now the gust were swelling, And the slant night-shower driving loud and fast! Those sounds which oft have raised me, whilst they 'awed, And sent my soul abroad, Might now perhaps their wonted impulse give, Might startle this dull pain, and make it move and live!

But, still the problem remains - the wind in <u>Part V</u> of "The Ancient Mariner" remains far off. If one looks ahead into <u>Part VI</u>, **stanzas** twelve and thirteen, one will discover that after "The curse is finally expiated," as the gloss explains, the wind does come and breathes directly on the Mariner, and only on him. The wind singles him out after the expiation of the curse, and he likens it to "a meadow-gale of spring. . . ." Perhaps the best way to think of the wind, therefore, in Part V, as it blows in the distant sky, is that it is the harbinger of the Mariner's further recovery and return home. The point at which the Mariner hears the wind in Part V is at a point something like a fourth or a third on his way to recovery. His redemption has at that time had a good beginning - he has been relieved of the Albatross, he has had gentle sleep, he has had the premonition in a dream of the breaking of the drought, and he has received the restoring rain - but many more happenings must yet become part of his experience.

The presence of a chorus of music within the province of the Mariner's recovery is not a surprising inclusion. Music is typically the language of joy and thanksgiving. The gloss that tells of the coming of "a blessed troop of angelic spirits, sent down by the invocation of the guardian saint" comes near the first of the **stanzas** that tell how the crew assemble around the mast and how music comes forth from them, though they are still only bodies. The angelic spirits help to celebrate the Mariner's salvation, and they so inspire him with their sounds that he is able to hear music in nature to which he has previously been oblivious - the songs of birds - and he is able after hearing their music to think of the noise of the sails in the terms of a "hidden brook / In the leafy month of June. . . ."

Music has a profound identification with inspiration in Coleridge's poetry. One need only think of the music of the Abyssinian maid in "Kubla Khan" for a vivid example, but he uses music both as subject matter and as metaphorical material almost countless times.

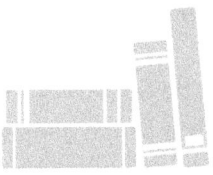

THE RIME OF THE ANCIENT MARINER

TEXTUAL ANALYSIS

PART VI

The advance of the action here is easier to follow than in the previous part of the poem. In Part VI the principal developments are these: the conversation between the two fellow-daemons of the Polar Spirit carries over from Part V, while the angelic power continues the thrust of the ship forward (during this time the Mariner remains in a trance); when the Mariner awakens out of the trance, he finds that the curse in the eyes of the dead men is still fixed on him; the spell is finally broken, and he feels the breeze on him; he arrives in the harbor of his own home and finds everything steeped in moonlight; the angelic spirits that have moved the limbs of the dead men leave the corpses; and the Pilot's boat comes out to the ship.

Stanzas one through six contain conversational exchange between the daemons; they are called in the text "First Voice" and "Second Voice." The fact that the First Voice speaks in sterner tones than does the Second Voice comes out in the first **stanza** of Part VI. The First Voice asks that the Second tell him with "soft response renewing" what gives the ship the power of movement. The final **stanza** of the preceding part has identified the softer tones of the Second Voice through the **simile** of honey-dew. The answer given by the Second Voice in **stanzas** two and three is that the Moon has power over the ocean and directs its movements: "For she guides him smooth or grim." He compares the ocean to a slave and the Moon to a lord: "'Still as a slave before his lord, / The ocean hath no blast. . . .'" But lines three and four of **stanza** three make the important discrimination that the character of the lord is of gracious spirit and disposition: "'. . . how graciously / She looketh down on him.'"

It is an excellent example of the splendid nuance of poetic figure that Coleridge as craftsman in poetry can accomplish when in **stanza** two he has the Second Voice describe the ocean's obedient, almost creaturely, dependence on the Moon for guidance. "'His [the ocean's] great bright eye most silently / Up to the Moon is cast - / If he may know which way to go. . . .'" One does not ordinarily think of a lord as female, especially when the subject is male, but such a relationship here gives the Moon not only the position of sovereign power but also presents the power in a loving and nourishing attitude, a combination of characteristics that we find really throughout the poem. Stanza four: the punitive First Voice cuts through again with his insistent questioning, almost as if he objected to the "extra" details about generosity in the Second Voice's answer; the First Voice does not seem to care so much about Love as he cares about Law: "'But why drives on that ship so fast, / Without or wave or wind?'"

The Second Voice gives his answer in **stanza** four in the simple nautical terms that any self-respecting daemon should know: "'The air is cut away before, / And closes from behind.'" He ends his answer with an exhortation to the daemon called the First Voice that they "'fly! more high, more high!'" so that they might not be belated (the word belated here may have some of the archaic association of "overtaken by night"), for when the Mariner awakens from his trance, the ship will move more slowly.

Straightforward, one-dimensional narration from the Mariner resumes in **stanza** seven. Perhaps the gloss should be read to clarify the first two lines of the **stanza**: "The supernatural motion is retarded; the Mariner awakes, and his penance begins anew." The Mariner relates his waking from the trance and his discovery that the ship was "sailing on / As in a gentle weather. . . ." The night was calm, and under the moon, high in the heavens, "The dead men stood together." He is reminded of the penance that weighs on him, and in **stanza** eight he reflects his internal attitudes of fear and dread toward the penance by commenting that the men were more fit for the tomb than for the deck of the ship. As their stony stare is fixed on him, the moonlight glitters in their eyes (glittering eyes again! a somewhat ambiguous figure in Coleridge, but always associated in some way with the supernatural).

The first main section of Part VI ends with **stanza** nine, in which the Mariner continues to tell of the enduring curse in the dead men's stare, and how he was so transfixed by it that he could not turn his eyes toward heaven in prayer.

At **stanza** ten the spell of the curse in the eyes of the dead men is broken, "The curse is finally expiated," and the Mariner looks out once more at the ocean, "the ocean green" (again that favorite color). The gripping fear that he has just felt, however, narrows his perspective, and he sees only a segment of what he might otherwise have seen. He explains the persistent terror of "The pang, the curse, with which the dead men died" in **stanza** eleven with that remarkable **simile** about the lonely walk that could not but touch the experience and engage the feeling of any reader:

Like one, that on a lonesome road Doth walk in fear and dread, And having once turned round walks on, And turns no more his head; Because he knows, a frightful fiend Doth close behind him tread.

Stanzas twelve through fourteen describe the wind that comes soon after the spell is broken. The Mariner's terror is abated by the ministry of the wind; and again there is the mysterious in its actions, for it touches only the Mariner. The wind (**stanza** twelve) has no sound and no motion and blows in no particular direction across the sea. Still (**stanza** thirteen) it raises the Mariner's hair, fans his cheek and mingles strangely with his fears, which is something like saying that he finds the wind a companion, nearly a compassionate friend. During the time that the wind is blessing the Mariner with its gentle, hopeful touch, the ship (**stanza** fourteen) is sailing swiftly, softly on.

Another of the abrupt transitions that characterize the poem throughout comes at **stanza** fifteen, which marks the next main section of Part VI and of the poem. The Mariner catches sight of his home port. His caution to believe in what his eyes reveal is evident in **stanzas** fifteen and sixteen. When he gets the first view of his "own countree," his exclamation is "Oh, dream of joy!" He fears it is only a vision, or that he only sleeps. Then (stanza fifteen) in a kind of process of elimination, he takes stock of the objects that have come in view. He names them off, but in the form of questions, no doubt going over in his mind whether they are truly the landmarks that mean home for him.

... is this indeed The light-house top I see? Is this the hill? is this the kirk? Is this mine own countree?

There is in the next **stanza**, stanza sixteen, the strongest statement of the Mariner's gladness. He is in his great joy moved to tears, and he prays that he might truly be awake in having the identifying landscape of his home before his eyes. If the Mariner were deluded and the story were rather that he was only seeing a mirage, this could be one of the most tragic and despairing scenes in literature. His prayer is that God will let it be true that he is seeing the very light-house, hill and kirk that belong to his home or that he may be granted the continuation of the delusion always.

The Mariner sails into the harbor-bay of home under the benign watchfulness of the Moon. The predominantly good associations of the Moon in the poem continue here, and it is the light of the Moon that unifies stanzas seventeen, eighteen, and nineteen. Notice the last two lines of stanza seventeen: "And on the bay the moonlight lay, / And the shadow of the Moon." Again, the last two lines of **stanza** eighteen: "The moonlight steeped in silentness The steady weathercock." And again, the first line of stanza nineteen: "And the bay was white with silent light. . . ."

But, **stanza** nineteen records also the disturbance of the "white . . . silent light" that lies on the harbor-bay. The stillness of the scene is broken by a changing spectrum of "crimson colors" on the water. The image that the Mariner sees is reflections, for when he out of curiosity about the disturbance turns around, he sees that the "many shapes, that shadows were" on the water are accounted for by the fact that the angelic spirits are leaving the bodies of the dead sailors. **Stanza** twenty tells of the shock he experienced when he beheld the sight:

A little distance from the prow Those crimson shadows were: I turned my eyes upon the deck - Oh, Christ! what saw I there!

The following three stanzas, stanzas twenty-one, twenty-two, and twenty-three, describe the angelic spirits as they "appear in their own forms of light." The Mariner tells (**stanza** twenty-one) how each of the bodies lay "flat" and "lifeless" on the deck, and how one of the angelic spirits stood on each one of the corpses. The Mariner vouches the honesty of his report by swearing "by the holy rood," that is by the cross of Christ. His first shock of terror at the sight is relieved in his heart when he sees (**stanza** twenty-two) the angelic spirits wave a blessing: "It was a heavenly sight! / They stood as signals to the land, / Each one a lovely sight. . . ." After their deep union of relationship through all the strange and torturing experiences of the voyage, there is now, as the spirits leave the dead bodies of the crew, a sense of regret in the Mariner's heart over their farewell. This regret comes through in **stanza** twenty-three when the Mariner tells that the spirits left without voice of sound, not speaking, only waving; he repeats "No voice" in line three, and then he uses interestingly an auditory image to describe the lack of sound:

This seraph band, each waved his hand, No voice did they impart - No voice; but oh! the silence sank Like music on my heart.

There is increasing joy. The last three **stanzas** of Part VI tell of the coming of the Pilot's boat to meet the Mariner's ship. When he hears the sound that the oars of the Pilot's boat make in the water, his eyes turn necessarily from the angelic spirits. In **stanza** twenty-four he hears the Pilot's greeting, and he sees the Pilot's boat. The Pilot and the Pilot's son approach the Mariner's ship with great speed, and the presence of the dead men on the deck around the Mariner is not enough to diminish the joy he feels at the coming of these human selves. It is after so long a time to be a reunion with the human community.

Part VI ends with a deep religious significance. The Mariner recognizes a third party in the approaching boat - it is the Hermit who lives in the wood and who is known for the loud singing of "godly hymns." The Mariner looks eagerly forward to the Hermit's shrieving him, that is, hearing his confession, granting him forgiveness in return, and washing the blood of the Albatross out of his soul.

Comment

There is rather obviously in the two voices in the end of Part V and in the beginning of Part VI the two sides of the Mariner's experience (and the two sides of the experience of every man), judgment and forgiveness. The First Voice is the spokesman for the judgment of God, the Second Voice the spokesman for the grace of God. Their conversation is essentially a conversation between Law and Love. The First Voice calls attention to the crime that the Mariner has committed, and he identifies himself with the avenging cause of the Polar Spirit. He asks his penal questions with a kind of staccato asperity. The Second Voice is "As soft as honey-dew," and it is the Second Voice that speaks, at the beginning of Part VI, of the Moon, that abiding source of love and redemption.

It may seem somewhat remarkable that the wind that comes finally to the Mariner is only a gentle breeze, "Like a meadow-gale of spring," for the kind of wind that Coleridge usually associates with emancipation from the deadening is a storm wind. If in Part V a roaring wind has careened about the sky, possibly forecasting the Mariner's growing emancipation, why would not a strong wind actually come now that his deliverance is more sure than ever? A roaring wind would be now appropriate to celebrate his retrieval from what seemed certain and lasting damnation. But, then, how much in keeping with the whole spirit of Part VI would a storm wind be? It is of all the parts of the poem the time of abiding grace, and although Coleridge would probably associate a storm wind with the free and powerful action of the imagination, redemption by grace is another thing. After what he has been through, it is hardly the time for the Mariner to be stirred by a driving storm of inspiration. He is in Part VI more perhaps than at any other time in the poem the creature in need of a divine blessing of gentle love and care. He is not in any position to be a creating force of the character of the dome-building poet in "Kubla Khan." And it is grace he receives; we may remind ourselves briefly of the events of grace in Part VI: the ocean looks up to the Moon for gracious care, in very nearly the way the Mariner later looks to God for the confirmation of his sighting of his home; the Second Voice, the more predominating of the two, speaks with grace in answer to the First Voice; the ship sails in gentle weather; the spell is broken; the gentle wind comes to the Mariner; the Mariner finds his home port in view; moonlight floods over every part of the scene; the seraph-band take leave with a blessing in their farewell gesture; the Pilot and the Pilot's boy bring renewal of human intercourse; the Mariner hears the Hermit singing hymns; finally, the Mariner has the blessed thought that the Hermit will grant him forgiveness, and the stain of his crime will be washed away.

There is a more frequent association in Coleridge's poetry of music with inspiration than there is of wind with inspiration. If at the last of Part VI, the Mariner were to hear the music of an Abyssinian maid, his response might be quite different. He might be transformed into a demon-god, creating by fiat, and consequently running the risk of further damnation for it. But, here, the hymns of the Hermit have the opposite effect: he is made more the humble creature than he was already, and he thinks not of rivaling the power of his Creator, but rather of seeking by way of the Hermit a portion of the power of forgiveness that can only belong to the Creator. If the young poet with flashing eyes and floating hair in "Kubla Khan" is identified with the First Adam, the Mariner is to be identified with Second Adam. The youthful poet gets an exorcism for his trouble; the Mariner finds salvation through grace.

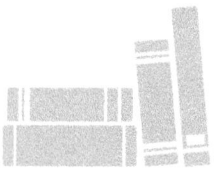

THE RIME OF THE ANCIENT MARINER

TEXTUAL ANALYSIS

PART VII

The skiff-boat carrying the Pilot, the Pilot's boy, and the Hermit draws near the ship. As they approach they all discuss the strange aspects of the Mariner's vessel, the now absent lights (which they had seen when the angelic spirits stood on the bodies of the dead crew members), the warped planks in the ship, the thin and sere sails. When the boat comes close the ship suddenly sinks as if it were lead, with "loud and dreadful sound." The Pilot falls down in his boat shrieking, the Hermit prays, the Pilot's boy becomes insane, the Mariner is thrown into the Pilot's boat and reaches land. The narrative ends when the Mariner asks the Hermit to shrieve him. From this point to the end, the Mariner informs the Wedding-Guest of the relationship between the events of his voyage and the fact that he must go on telling his story, as he has told it to him. He makes several comments in a wistful and nostalgic manner about life in community with human beings, a contrast to the life of wandering that his penance has imposed on him. He concludes his address to the Wedding-Guest with a brief sermon about how the man who hopes to pray well must love all creation as closely as he can to the way in which God loves it. The poem ends with the Wedding-Guest going forth from the Mariner, sadder for what he has heard but also wiser.

Part VII opens with a further description of the Hermit. He is in a sense the most fully characterized figure in the poem, even more than the Mariner himself. Three **stanzas** are given to an objective portrayal of him (stanza twenty-six in Part VI and **stanzas** one and two in Part VII), and he speaks for two **stanzas** (stanzas four and five in Part VII). One can think of him as a domestic Mariner; he loves to hear the adventures of others, but he can in his home-bound piety experience adventure only in a vicarious way: "He loves to talk with marineres / That come from a far countree." (**stanza** one) But there is the compensation for his land-limited existence of having hymns that he can believingly sing and prayers ("He kneels at morn, and noon, and eve. . . .") that he can trust, a security that comes from deep involvement in home, in the human community, and in dependable fact.

The brief digression on the character and religious practices of the Hermit ends with **stanza** two, and the Mariner takes up again the narration of what happened to the ship as it sailed into the harbor. He tells of the conversation of the three persons in the boat as they rowed nearer and nearer; this conversation occupies in the text **stanzas** two, three, four, and five. The Pilot speaks in **stanza** three and comments on the extinguished lights that had been formerly so conspicuous on the ship. They had taken them to be clear, bright signal lights. The Hermit (**stanzas** four and five) agrees with the Pilot that it is strange (he vows by his faith) that the lights have gone out and strange also that the crew on the ship had made no response to their greeting.

He comments on the parched and buckled wood of the ship and the dried up (sere) sails. His figure of comparison drawn from nature (almost an epic **simile**) shows Coleridge's sense of discernment for mood and feel in natural phenomena at its most sophisticated level (helped some, perhaps, by Dorothy Wordsworth):

'... and see those sails, How thin they are and sere! I never say aught like to them, Unless perchance it were Brown skeletons of leaves that lag My forest-brook along; When the ivy-tod is heavy with snow, And the owlet whoops to the wolf below, That eats the she-wolf's young.'

A comparison in courage between the Pilot and the Hermit comes in stanza six, between the honest, well-intentioned man (the Pilot) and the man of faith (the Hermit). The Pilot expresses fear at the "fiendish look" of the ship, but the Hermit replies to him "cheerily," "'Push on, push on.'"

The sinking of the ship begins in the last line of **stanza** seven, and the account of that event continues through **stanza** ten. The first sound connected with the sinking is heard (**stanza** seven) as the skiff-boat comes "close beneath the ship. . . ." The ship is actually sunk by a sound. No facts are given as to the origin of the sound. It begins "Under the water," becomes dreadfully loud, reaches the ship, splits the bay - and the ship sinks. The only other circumstance that we are told about it is that it is thunderous enough to smite the sky and ocean (**stanza** nine) and to resound from the surrounding hill (**stanza** ten). The Mariner finds himself mysteriously buoyed up on the waters of the harbor and then equally mysteriously placed in the Pilot's boat (**stanza** nine). The end of the chronicle of the sinking ship is in **stanza** ten.

Stanzas eleven and twelve reveal the various responses of those in the boat, the Mariner, the Pilot, the Pilot's boy, the Hermit, to this weird, dismaying kaleidoscope of events. The Mariner is so stunned by his fantastic transit from ship to boat that he can only move his lips. The Pilot is thrown into a paroxysm of terror and falls down into the boat. The Hermit raises his eyes in prayer. The Pilot's boy becomes insane. It is easy to miss the first part of line one in **stanza** twelve; the Mariner tells that he took the oars. This, of course, explains the mad accusation that the Pilot's boy makes in the last lines of **stanza** twelve - he thinks the Mariner is the Devil: "Ha! ha!' quoth he, 'full plain I see, / The Devil knows how to row.' "

Stanzas thirteen and fourteen close the narrative. The Mariner steps out of the boat onto the soil of his homeland, and then asks for the Hermit's absolution: "'O shrieve me, shrieve me, holy man!'" But the Hermit being also somewhat dumbfounded by all that he has been a witness to can scarcely wait to ask the Mariner who he really is; perhaps he also suspects that the Mariner is not a "normal" seaman, that what has happened has been too super-natural to trust. The Hermit grants the Mariner's request for absolution in something like one second (the whole absolution takes one line), and then with insistence says, "'Say quick, . . . I bid thee say - / What manner of man art thou?'"

The Mariner's "penance of life" is the subject of the following three stanzas, stanzas fifteen, sixteen, and seventeen. The facts of his penance are briefly these: 1) the first evidence of the penance was great physical pain; 2) this "woful agony" caused him to begin telling his strange story; 3) he learned that when he told it he was relieved of suffering; 4) at undetermined times the pain starts again within him and continues until he has repeated the tale; 5) he goes from place to place with a "strange power of speech," and 6) he knows through an unexplainable perception who the person is that must hear him.

There has been a good deal of critical discussion of the way in which the Mariner is a near perfect embodiment of the Romantic **theme** of solitude. Whether one takes this matter seriously or not, the character of the Mariner as outcast, as wanderer, as isolato, finds a vivid delineation against the background merriment of the wedding, from which the Wedding-Guest has been detained. The first stage of the delineation is that abrupt transition between **stanza** seventeen and eighteen. Immediately after the Mariner confesses to the Wedding-Guest that he must go on indefinitely repeating his "ghastly tale," there is the concussion of sound from the wedding festival. The transition is abrupt again when after this **stanza** of "wedding guests," the bride in the garden bower, the singing of the bride-maids, and the vesper bell, the Mariner proclaims his solitude:

O Wedding-Guest! this soul hath been Alone on a wide wide sea: So lonely 'twas, that God himself Scarce seemed there to be.

A third abrupt transition is at the beginning of the next **stanza**, for there, immediately after the Mariner's loneliness is put very nearly in the terms of Christ on the cross who feared that God had forsaken him, immediately after, attention is turned to the joyous marriage-feast, but to the marriage-feast only in process to the even deeper communal values of church (kirk), friends (loving friends), and the worship of God in fellowship with the whole human company.

So many marked transitions coming consecutively can hardly be passed over as mere happenstance of subject or composition. Besides, abrupt transitions occur so frequently throughout the poem that their use becomes an obviously conscious literary technique.

The famous moral to (to more than of) the poem, famous not out of the degree of acceptance it has been accorded, famous not for the extent to which it so harmoniously accords with the poem as a whole, but famous in the sense of its having been made the subject of so many critical discussions, the moral comes in **stanzas** twenty-two and twenty-three. The purpose of the moral seems to be to help the creature find a richer, more profound prayer relationship with God. It is about prayer: "He prayeth well, who loveth well. . . ."; "He prayeth best, who loveth best. . . ." The structure and tone of these two **stanzas** would seem to mean that the whole of the Mariner's story leads naturally, perhaps inevitably, to his proclaiming this message: if you want to be related meaningfully with God in prayer, then love His creation, all of it "man and bird and beast" - in a way that as closely as possible copies the way God loves His creation. That is, if you want to pray well, love the creation; the reason for loving the creation is that God loves it.

The Wedding-Guest is "A sadder and a wiser man" for having heard the Mariner's story, though it was not for the purpose of improving his education that he listened to the Mariner, for we know he listened because he had to: he was constrained against his will. There is a kind of ambiguity - not surprising in this poem, to be sure - about the Wedding-Guest's greater wisdom at the end. Are we to understand that he is "sadder and . . . wiser" when he wakes the following day because of the way the Mariner exhorts him to live, that is because he knows that he cannot really live in keeping with the Mariner's moral? Or is he "sadder and . . . wiser" the next day because when he left the Mariner at the end of the Mariner's tale "He went like one that hath been stunned, / And is of sense forlorn"? Or is it because the Mariner's moral did not really mean that much to him, considering the grimness of the story, that is, that the moral was more perplexing than helpful coming at the end of a story that would probably not leave most people in any frame of mind to consider how to learn to pray better? Whatever result the whole experience had on the Wedding-Guest's life, he did not begin immediately loving God's creation, "man and bird and beast." He does not go to join the joyful wedding party; rather, he turns from the bridegroom's door.

Comment

The ship is sunk by sound. It is tempting to think of the universe that groans in all its parts that Paul describes to the Romans, chapter 8. Paul's doctrine of creation was, of course, that the creation fell when man fell, that sin did not affect only the creature but extended to all creation, not only affecting but infecting. This is to say that when man sinned and fell out of right relationship with God, the creation - all of it - fell out of right relationship also, at the same time. John Donne picks up this idea and develops it in his poem "An Anatomy of the World." It may not be too great an exaggeration to think of Coleridge as having the ship sunk by this primordial groan: the sound is encompassing of the whole world around the ship - it begins under the ship, splits the bay, smites the sky and ocean (which is pretty inclusive) and then resounds from the surrounding hill.

It is not evident within the structure of the story why the Pilot's boy should become mad, or to go further, why there should be a pilot's boy at all. There is the possible explanation, of course, that he is simply there to add interesting variety to the happenings. Is he only decoration? Some critics have discussed the possibility that he is a scapegoat of sorts, a sacrificial animal onto which is loaded the Mariner's sin and then sent off into the wilderness of insanity.

The moral of "The Ancient Mariner" has troubled most of us, mainly because we cannot really be content with the Mariner's parting words as a moral to which we would be compelled by the events of his story, or that we would find unquestionably corroborated by reviewing this tale of foolish crime and inevitable punishment. Usually included in any discussion of the moral is a comment that H. N. Coleridge collected in Specimens of the Table Talk of the late Samuel Taylor Coleridge. Coleridge is supposed to have said on one occasion about the poem,

Mrs. Barbauld once told me that she admired the Ancient Mariner very much, but that there were two faults in it, - it was improbable, and had no moral. As for the probability, I owned that that might admit some question; but as to the want of a moral, I told her that in my own judgment the poem had too much; and that the only, or chief fault, if I might say so, was the obtrusion of the moral sentiment so openly on the reader as a principle or cause of action in a work of such pure imagination. It ought to have had no more moral than the Arabian Night's tale of the merchant's sitting down to eat dates by the side of a well, and throwing the shells aside, and lo! a genie starts up, and says he must kill the aforesaid merchant because one of the date shells had, it seems, put out the eye of the genie's son.

This statement by Coleridge about the moral in the poem may only lead to confusion worse confounded. In a true sense, Coleridge's statement only attests the caprice at the heart of the poem, that what the Mariner does when he kills the Albatross is as haphazard as is the whole encounter between the merchant with the genie. Taken this way Coleridge's comment about

Mrs. Barbauld's criticism would mean that the moral of the poem is that the human creature is subject in this cosmos to forces beyond himself over which he has no control. That is, shoot a bird and get exile for life! Eat a date and throw down a shell, and you get death! If one interprets Coleridge's statement this way, the moral is in the action of the poem, not in that too pious-sounding "tag" at the end about loving all things and finding consequently a rich relationship with God. The moral, consequently, that Coleridge is referring to is not the little sermon in **stanzas** twenty-two and twenty-three in Part VII for the very obvious reason that the story of the merchant and the genie could not lead one to the conclusion that if one loves God's creation as closely as possible to the way He loves it, one will find prayer meaningful. The moral of the Arabian Night's tale would not lead one to affirm that ". . . the dear God who loveth us,/He made and loveth all."

The events that the ancient Mariner tells the Wedding-Guest about could not prepare him to accept a moral that so much presupposes the freedom of the human will. If *"The Rime of the Ancient Mariner"* is about anything, it is about the lack of freedom of the will, whether this results in a philosophy of Fate in the Greek sense or in a theology of Providence in the Hebraic sense. The problem in the poem, the central problem, is that the creature has not enough control over himself to be able to love God's creation, even if in a kind of intellectual way he wanted to. Coleridge of all people would be aware of those dimensions of darkness in the human self that can so easily swallow up the brightness of intention, however bright. His poems are full of the ambiguity of motive, of the ambivalence in the human self. Beyond his poetry, his notebooks are in numerous places the diary of a man looking with unashamed scrutiny at the darkness in himself, darkness in those things in which he would hope with all his heart to be most pure.

One can read the Mariner's two-stanza moral at the end of the poem as very nearly intended contrast with the story he has related. The Wedding - Guest might very well go away stunned, forlorn of sense, because he realized that the Mariner's moral sharpened the facts of the unmanageable caprice of human actions and the unmanageable caprice of the forces that come to bear on human existence. After the kinds of experiences the Mariner talks about, one would perhaps be stunned at the idea of even attempting prayer to God. One would be much more prone to speak and act as Melville's Captain Ahab does. The only thing that saves the Mariner from finding a Moby Dick to hunt down is that he can disperse, parcel out, his fury on such subjects as the Wedding - Guest. It might be a penance, his traveling from land to land and telling his tale, but then it might be the only way that an ancient Mariner could stay alive - to draw others into recognizing the agony and loneliness he has known. This is probably the only way poets can live, and, of course, many poets do not live very long because of what they have seen and heard and because of the way they must behave as a consequence of their peculiar kind of seeing and hearing.

THE RIME OF THE ANCIENT MARINER

ESSAY QUESTIONS AND ANSWERS

Question: What kind of poem is "The Rime of the Ancient Mariner" from the point of view of structure and style?

Answer: The poem is written as a **ballad**, in the general form of the traditional **ballad** of medieval or early Elizabethan times. Coleridge uses the **ballad stanza**, a four-line stanza, rhyming a b c b, but he varies it considerably, with some **stanzas** extending up to nine lines. He is able to achieve a richer, more sweeping sense of the supernatural through these expansions; he is able to move beyond the more domesticated kind of supernaturalism of the homey four-line stanza.

He starts with the usual **ballad stanza** in the first of the poem, in order to make the reader acquainted with the verse form and with the poetic ethos of "The Rime of the Ancient Mariner." These early **stanzas** seem to anchor the reader's mind. But in the twelfth **stanza**, the pattern changes to a a a b c b. By this time the reader has become at home in the poem. Interestingly, the change occurs, certainly by Coleridge's deliberate intent, at the point in the poem when the Wedding-Guest makes his last major protest to the Mariner. The action of the voyage is about to begin. One example of the variation of the **ballad** form is that Coleridge throughout the poem will occasionally insert a line that does nothing to further the story (see **stanza** three, Part II) but that enriches the emotional texture of the poem.

Coleridge's attraction to the **ballad** form was probably owing in great measure to the liberation it afforded him from the confines of modern life, a freedom it gave him to move spaciously within the unbounded areas of imaginative creation.

Question: To what extent is the Mariner believable as a character? Does he have the authenticity of identity that a reader would desire?

Answer: There is certainly behind the character of the Mariner in the poem the traditional story of the Wandering Jew, a figure that had considerable influence on Romantic literature, used by P. B. Shelley, for example, in the accounts of Ahasuerus in Queen Mab and the Revolt of Islam. The story has a Jewish tradesman refusing Jesus a moment of rest as He carried His cross to Golgotha; the Jew receives consequently condemnation to life-in death. He is condemned to wandering from place to place, where he must tell of his sin until the Second Coming of Christ. Coleridge used the story again in "The Wanderings of Cain."

William Wordsworth was among the first to say that the Mariner has no character. But Charles Lamb, another contemporary of Coleridge, said the ancient Mariner as a character with feelings, faced with such happenings as the poem tells about, "dragged [him] along like Tom Piper's magic whistle." John Livingston Lowes in more recent times spoke of the real **protagonists** in the poem as the elements, Earth, Air, Fire, and Water.

Irving Babbit echoed Wordsworth's criticism in saying that the Mariner does not do anything in the poem beyond shooting the Albatross, that the Mariner does not really act, but is acted upon only, and that the Mariner is an incarnation of the Romantic concern with the solitary. George Herbert Clarke has interpreted the ancient Mariner to be at one and the same time himself as a real character in the poem, Samuel Taylor Coleridge, and all men; the Mariner is Representative Man, sinning, being punished, being redeemed.

One possibility, perhaps the best one, is to consider the Mariner as poet more than character in the sense in which we associate "personality" with characters in literature. As a poet who speaks ("I have strange power of speech. . . ."), he does not have the obligation of a character to act. The poem should not be read really with the expectation with which one reads a novel. The Mariner is not what he is because he is involved with other human beings - but because he is alone.

Question: What symbolic purpose does the Albatross serve in the poem?

Answer: This is a much debated question. One critic, Mr. George Whalley, has discussed the Albatross as a symbol of the creative imagination, and he makes this interpretation by way of associating the Albatross with the wind, because the Mariner "killed the bird / That made the breeze to blow." (Whalley's italics.) Whalley notes that the bird is often in literature associated with imagination or inspiration. Professor Kathleen Coburn in her editing of Coleridge's notebooks comments on the frequency with which Coleridge uses bird images for himself. There is certainly much cause for taking Whalley seriously. The Albatross is undoubtedly more than a piece of stage property.

John Livingston Lowes has spoken of the function of the Albatross as a unifying agent in the poem, binding together the voyage, the supernatural happenings, and the process of punishment that the Mariner must undergo; these, he says, are the principal structural elements in the work.

G. W. Knight in The Starlit Dome stresses that the Albatross is greeted as "a Christian soul," and that the bird can suggest a force of redemption in creation such as Christ is confessed to be. The Albatross like Christ could be interpreted as leading man from his primitive origins to moral and spiritual improvement. The fact that the Albatross is hung around the Mariner's neck (rather than a cross) may suggest the death of Christ.

Robert Penn Warren directs attention to the way the killing of the Albatross in the poem is the compromising of the sacred values of hospitality; the Mariner "inhospitably killeth the pious bird of good omen." The killing of the Albatross becomes then symbolically a murder, for the bird loved the man who killed it. Because the crime has no motive, it has, Mr. Warren decides, symbolic connections with the original Fall of man. He points out a cluster of associations with the wind (creative force), the Albatross (friend and companion), and Mariner (imagination). The killing of the Albatross has gravity far beyond cruelty to animals - it is Original Sin.

W. H. Auden relates the Albatross to the symbol of the Holy Ghost in Christian theology, the Dove, and then through the whiteness of the Dove to the White Lamb, Christ.

Humphry House says that the prose gloss when added to the appearance, the character, and the power of the bird in the poem makes the killing of the Albatross as great as the murder of a human being. He calls attention to all the human acts in which the bird is associated in the poem: the Christian greeting; the friendly, trusting response of the Albatross; the sharing of food; the play between bird and crew. The Mariner's crime is a crime against the most precious qualities of humanity.

Question: What is the type of religious consciousness that pervades "The Ancient Mariner"?

Answer: The most conspicuous elements of religious faith in the poem are those of Medieval Catholicism: the Virgin Mary, the petitions to saints, and the practices of confession and absolution. But the poem is permeated with religious ideas and religious feeling in a much larger sense. There are daemons and spirits, representations of religious consciousness in a much too primitive sense to be circumscribed within the bounds of any one denominational framework. In this regard, it is remarkable that when Coleridge talks about the moral in the poem (in reply to Mrs. Barbauld), he does so not with reference to Medieval Catholicism nor to Biblical Faith nor to Protestant Christianity, but, rather, with reference to a story in the Arabian Nights, hardly a religious story in any orthodox sense.

For a young man who was very close to the consideration of the Unitarian ministry as a vocation during the time that he was writing "The Ancient Mariner," the use of such elements from Medieval Catholicism may seem odd, particularly when that young man could probably dislike nothing more than the Church of Rome, unless it were the French nation. But, remember that he is writing a poem, a consciously executed literary work, and that it is necessary for him therefore to subdue his personal preferences (and prejudices) to his larger artistic purposes. The theology of Medieval Catholicism with its gracious Virgin, its saints, and its absolutions, would more quickly suggest to the reader's mind a world of supernatural happenings than would Unitarian Christianity with its plain meeting houses, its concern with social reform, and its rational God.

Still, Coleridge in writing the poem does not stop being what he is as a person with ideas and attitudes. The basic theology in the poem, the pervading theological understanding underneath the trappings of Medieval Catholicism, is that of the Protestant Reformation generally and that of John Calvin more particularly (however, one may take Calvinistic theology and with certain clever, though ultimately dishonest, maneuvers turn it into a Greek scheme of Fate). The world in which the Mariner has lived during the experiences that his story is about is more a nightmare world than it isn't. But, then, whenever the Sovereignty of God, the God to Whom the Biblical Scriptures make testimony, is made ultimate and man's will is in all things made subject to His Will, any world can become a nightmare world, and usually does. This is why the moral "tag" in the last Part of the poem is in line with the business of those inane sermons that say, "Love God and be happy." "The Ancient Mariner" is for one thing about the fact that if one loves God one most likely will be miserable. Because God does not make explanations usually for what he does, at least not in the terms that humans would consider intelligent, one may find himself living in a world where his best efforts at rationality are foolish, considering the terms in which the God Who Acts is acting. There is through all of the Bible the **theme** of God's wisdom making man's wisdom foolish. Coleridge was haunted by the fact: his poems (to say nothing of notebooks and letters) continually show the disturbance.

Despite the fact that Coleridge was a Unitarian and as such would have put the emphasis on man's resources to improve himself morally, and consequently to improve the world in which man lives, he was probably more Calvinistic in his basic theological orientation than he was Unitarian (although in a sense anything that was at odds with the Church of England at the time was called Unitarian). Coleridge was too much aware of the fundamental and inevitable blackness in man's nature ever to be an unfettered optimist, although he did do a great deal of loud talking about his belief in man's inevitable moral improvement.

In summary, the "religious" world of "The Ancient Mariner" is the world of an omniscient, omnipotent God and the world of His creatures, suffering severely, doubting horribly, humiliated unbearably under His Sovereign Godhood - but still in their hearts hoping unceasingly. The world of "The Ancient Mariner" is in its foundations the world of Old Testament relations with God, New Testament redemption in Christ, and Protestant belief in what is in the categories of the world's wisdom the absurd. "The Ancient Mariner" can be one of the most important of Coleridge's poems for the study of the tumultuous ebb and flow of his theological thinking during the last years of the seventeen - hundreds.

CHRISTABEL

INTRODUCTION

DATE

Coleridge probably began writing "Christabel" in 1798. However, Arthur H. Nethercot in his book-length study of the poem, *The Road to Tryermaine*, questions Coleridge's dating. He mentions, and not without good reason, Coleridge's tendency to confuse dates, often to his own advantage.

Robert Southey wished to publish "Christabel" in the 1800 edition of his *Annual Anthology*. Coleridge on 15 October 1799 agreed to try to finish the poem for this edition, but on 10 November he wrote to Southey explaining that he did not think the poem should appear at the first of the volume, as Southey wished. Coleridge tried again in 1800 to finish the poem, looking toward its publication in the 1800 edition of *Lyrical Ballads*. But "Christabel" remained a fragment. A letter from Coleridge to James Webbe Tobin 17 September 1800, gives a most significant revelation of his feelings toward the poem:

The delay in Copy has been owing in part to me, as the writer of "Christabel" - Every line has been produced by me with labor-pangs. I abandon Poetry altogether - I leave the higher & deeper Kinds to Wordsworth, the delightful, popular & simply dignified to Soughey; & reserve for myself the honorable attempt to make others feel and understand their writings, as they deserve to be felt & understood

(*Collected Letters*, I, Letter 351)

Nevertheless the poem had reached such lengths by 10 October that Wordsworth felt it was too long for the *Lyrical Ballads*. Only a few days later he wrote to Thomas Poole, "The truth is, the endeavor to finish "Christabel", (which has swelled into a Poem of 1400 lines) for the second Volume of the *Lyrical* **Ballads** threw my business terribly back. . . ." These statements from Coleridge strongly suggest that we have only a part of the original poem, only 677 lines, although the poem in whatever number of lines it reached was still fragmentary. Coleridge had projected five books for the poem.

"Christabel" was circulated privately and given special readings before its publication on 25 May 1816. Among those who read it aloud on special occasions were Walter Scott, Wordsworth, and Byron. In August of 1816 and again in January of 1821, Coleridge spoke of his hope to finish "Christabel." Three years before his death Coleridge is reported to have said about his not finishing the poem,

The reason of my not finishing "Christabel" is not, that I don't know how to do it - for I have, as I always had, the whole plan entire from beginning to end in my mind; but I fear I could not carry on with equal success the execution of the idea, an extremely subtle and difficult one.

WHAT KIND OF STORY IS "CHRISTABEL"?

"Christabel" is more at home in the literature of medieval romance than in any other **genre**. It is in part a story of innocent love surrounded by and threatened by inscrutable forces within man, particularly that kind of sexual irrationality that produces situations and incidents not explainable in the usual terms of rational human intelligence. The mystery of inner motive and outer action, particularly with regard to man's sexual self, is a frequent **theme** in medieval romances and ballads. One so often finds in medieval literature stories of witches and fairies used as vehicles for expression of the mystery, and the women in the stories are often described in words that have not only ancient but modern sexual connotations, "enchanting," "charming," "bewitching." The women in these medieval stories, like Geraldine, are young and beautiful, although their beauty is often a camouflage for the evil, hideous creatures that they are in their essential inner selves. Comment has often been made on the way in which Geraldine is in the line of witches that includes Spenser's Duessa, Acrasia, and Phaedria. But, although "Christabel" belongs generally in this **genre**, the poem is too complex in its exploration of character and human motive to be confined by it: Christabel as a character is not all good, and Geraldine is not all evil.

STRUCTURE

There are two parts in the poem as we have it; as discussed above there may have been more. "The Conclusion to Part II," often discussed as a critical problem, seems to have little relationship to the narrative of the poem, although it probably has a profound relationship of another kind.

The story of "Christabel" is told by a narrator who bears no such close relationship to the events he describes as that of the ancient Mariner. This dramatic speaker in "Christabel" takes no part in the events he reports, and although he can make certain comments of his own on what is happening, he is not able to unfold the inner mind of the characters he talks about. Another fact about the narrator's role in the poem is that he assumes from time to time the first person form of address and therefore enters into a certain intimacy of relationship with the reader. There is probably a greater credibility in the poem because of the narrator's stance. On the whole, he tells the story as a detached observer.

CHARACTER AND THEME

There are four characters in "Christabel." They are Christabel, Geraldine, Sir Leoline, and Bracy the bard. The two principal characters are Christabel and Geraldine, Geraldine probably the **protagonist**, Christabel the antagonist. The main action of the poem would seem to be centered around Christabel, although Geraldine is probably the character who makes the poem move; the poem is for us as readers "successful" according to whether we, like Christabel, are seduced. Both Christabel and Geraldine are studies in good and evil. Christabel is ambiguous in her goodness, as Geraldine is ambiguous in her evil. Christabel's innocence and virtue are often praised by the narrator, and these qualities are heightened by his obvious fear for her welfare, as if the good were continuously threatened by the evil, and as if the good were not able to protect itself in the hostile surroundings of the world. (In a deeper sense, however, these attitudes on the part of the narrator may draw us into a more penetrating study of Christabel, not just as the innocent maiden threatened by antagonistic and corrupting forces without, but as a complex human being, possessing, for all her innocence, some of the darkness within that exists without.) Of course, it is a strategically placed affirmation of her goodness that at the very beginning of the poem she is found in prayer. The narrator often makes prayerful interjections in her behalf, for example, "Jesu, Maria, shield her well." The epithet "sweet" for Christabel is frequent in the poem.

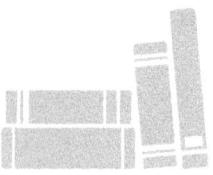

ANALYSIS OF THE POEM CHRISTABEL

TEXTUAL ANALYSIS

PART I

PART I, LINES 1 - 22

The time of the first setting is midnight. The castle clock strikes the hour. The "Tu-whit!-Tu-whoo!" of the owls has awakened the cock that now crows drowsily. The castle is that of the wealthy, aged knight, Sir Leoline. The old watchdog that belongs to him has a peculiar habit of echoing the clock as it strikes the times of the midnight hour: this "toothless mastiff bitch" utters short, muted howls, one howl for each quarter hour, and twelve for the full hour. Some people say that the dog can see the shroud of Sir Leoline's wife, who died years ago while giving birth to Christabel.

The setting is an April night, still cold from winter's influence, for the spring comes slowly to the area of the land where the castle is located. Coleridge's all-important moon-effects are working here. There is a full moon, but its mystery is emphasized in there being a "thin gray cloud" that robes the sky and the moon, and that causes the full moon to appear "both small and dull." The atmosphere of the poem is established in these opening lines: throughout the poem it is an atmosphere both chill and gray.

Comment

Midnight is, of course, the setting for many so-called Gothic stories. One may find many elements in "Christabel" familiar to the Gothic type. It is important to see, however, the way in which Coleridge takes familiar machinery and adapts it to his profounder purposes. "Christabel" is not just another Gothic tale, although it shows the influence of such Gothic writers as Mrs. Ann Radcliffe, who remained Coleridge's favorite among the group; Coleridge had, in fact, written a review of her romance *The Mysteries of Udolpho* in *The Critical Review* for August, 1794. "Christabel" is a severe, and as far as it goes, a relentless study of good and evil.

Coleridge employs an echo technique in the poem. There is the crowing of the cock in answer to the hoot of the owls; there is the barking of the mastiff bitch in answer to the clock. There will be other echo effects later in the poem. Neither the owl nor the cock has been in folklore associated with the benign. But there is of the two the greater peril in the crowing of the cock in the middle of the night. There is in these early lines the insinuation of the evil that will soon be substantiated in the interaction between Geraldine and Christabel. It is obvious that Coleridge through his narrative comments on the atmosphere and happenings around the castle intends to build the effect of mystery and strangeness. He better inspires that "willing suspension of disbelief for the moment, which constitutes poetic faith" by having the narrator attribute to others the idea of the dog's being able to see the lady's shroud.

PART I, LINES 23 - 36

Christabel, the lovely daughter of Sir Leoline, has been disturbed in her sleep by thoughts of her lover, the knight to whom she is betrothed. She has gone into the forest, about a furlong from the castle. There she will pray for her absent lover. The forest into which she goes is dead; nature is dead here; this is a forest in which nothing is green with life except a parasitic growth, mistletoe, and a kind of plant life that feeds off decaying wood, moss.

Comment

The condition of death that exists in the natural setting into which Christabel goes is intended to intensify the foreboding quality in these early lines of the poem. Coleridge returns to the sterility of the setting in lines 45 - 52.

PART I, LINES 36 - 57

Christabel is startled by a moaning sound from the other side of the oak tree, underneath which she prays. She has no idea of what the source of the moan is. The narrator (line 53) interjects a prayer to the Virgin Mary for Christabel's safety, "Jesu, Maria, shield her well!" Christabel goes with folded arms to the other side of the oak tree to investigate the sound she has heard.

Comment

As soon as Coleridge has introduced the danger of Christabel's situation in the forest (and the word "moaned" contributes to this feeling of danger), he returns immediately for eleven lines to the deadness of the scene. There is not enough wind in the forest to move a ringlet of Christabel's hair and not enough to stir the "one red leaf, the last of its clan," to which the narrator (we may call him a "dramatic speaker") carefully calls attention. Note the words here: "chill," "bear," "moaneth bleak."

Naturally the narrator would pray to the Virgin, for the setting is that of a medieval castle. As in "The Rime of the Ancient Mariner," the supernatural is more evident in the machinery of Medieval Catholicism - prayers to the Virgin, references to saints, and the presence of various physical objects that have religious meanings. Statues of the Virgin, of the saints, beads for the rosary, medals, candles, and other such gear, help in religious settings to give tangible quality to the supernatural. Coleridge would, of course, given his fierce Protestant thrust, find in his own faith and attitudes such paraphernalia, and any such intention to give form to the supernatural, utterly repugnant. But, then, he has an artistic purpose in "Christabel," and he must as an artist subdue his own personal orientations to his creation of art. The more stark theological and ecclesiastical emphases of the Protestant Reformation would not permit the kinds of enchanting effects that Coleridge achieves in "Christabel" through the use of the Medieval Catholic setting. Too, even more obviously, at the time of the setting of the poem, Luther had not yet taken up nails and hammer in Wittenberg, and John Calvin was yet to find his way to Geneva.

With further attention to the narrator's role, it is, as suggested before, his relationship to the events he describes, and his relation to his listener (the reader), that provide one of the best ways for Coleridge to make the supernatural believable, to accomplish that "transfer from our inward nature a human interest and a semblance of truth sufficient to procure for these shadows of imagination that willing suspension of disbelief for the moment, which constitutes poetic faith." We may observe in the lines here under consideration that he seems in his descriptions of the scene to be very familiar with the area in which the castle of Sir Leoline is located. He describes the oak tree with several well-chosen details, and earlier he was shown himself to be familiar with the seasons in this vicinity and with the lore of Sir Leoline's household - for one thing that it is said the dog can see the shroud of Sir Leoline's deceased wife.

PART I, LINES 58 - 70

Christabel finds on the other side "Of the huge, broad-breasted, old oak tree" a stately, richly-clad lady, "Beautiful exceedingly!" Christabel is, of course, startled by her, for nothing could be so unlikely as finding such a lady in a dim forest at midnight. Christabel does first what is most natural for her to do -she prays to the Virgin for protection, and then she asks the lady who she is.

Comment

Attention has already been called to the degree of emphasis placed on Geraldine's attire. Indeed one very strong reason for Christabel's being startled was that Geraldine was "so richly clad." There is much about her to give her the appearance of brightness. Geraldine is "a damsel bright," she is "Drest in a silken robe of white," she is standing in the moonlight, her "arms were bare," and gems in her hair glittered wildly in the moonlight. She is just what we would expect Christabel to be. Perhaps they are not so different; perhaps they are intended to be two sides of the same psyche.

Christabel's virtue is again emphasized in her prayers, and there is the narrator's fear for the safety of trusting goodness in this potentially dangerous situation. And again Christabel's virtue is apparent in her naivete: besides having gone into the forest alone, she does not flee at the strange sound she hears; she does just what any smart, aware person would not do. Many of the remarks of the narrator are about Christabel's goodness and innocence.

PART I, LINES 71 - 103

This part of the poem contains Geraldine's account of her distress. She tells (1) that she is "of a noble line," (2) that her name is Geraldine, (3) that she, "a maid forlorn," was abducted the morning before by five warriors that she did not know, (4) that they tied her on a white horse and followed her on their own white horses (of course the horses would have to be white) at a furious pace, having smothered her resistance through threats and constraint, (5) that they flew through the night to this place, where the tallest of the warriors (appropriate for a stately lady like Geraldine) took her from the paltry, (6) that she has been here for a length of time that she cannot recall, for she has been entranced part of the time, (7) that the warrior who placed her beneath the oak swore they would return hastily, and (8) that she is in a miserable state and needs Christabel's help in order to escape.

Comment

One thing becomes increasingly obvious, particularly on a second reading of the poem: Geraldine is eager to have physical contact with Christabel. She twice asks Christabel to stretch forth her hand to help her. In her first speech she begs (line 75), "Stretch forth thy hand, and have no fear!" Then again at the end of the brief story that she tells of her experiences she says to Christabel (lines 102 - 103), "Stretch forth thy hand (thus ended she), / And help a wretched maid to flee." Perhaps there is in Geraldine the hope that contact with such a maiden as Christabel will redeem her evil nature and relieve her misery. This theory is substantiated by much of the folklore about vampires, of which Geraldine is a type. Nethercot in his review of vampire legends in *The Road to Tryermaine* cites an article form 1896 on a type of vampire that can suck out the strength of a person, not in the more familiarly fantasied way of sucking the person's blood, but, rather, in the sapping of psychic strength. There are a number of places in "Christabel" where Geraldine cannot go on without some contact with Christabel. The faintness of Geraldine when Christabel first meets her suggests most immediately a great fatigue in her. Her voice when she first speaks is "faint and sweet." She says (line 74) "I scarce can speak for weariness." But we know about Geraldine what Christabel does not know, and this claim to fatigue is only a first step in Geraldine's program to seduce Christabel to some selfish purpose. There are too many statements and suggestions in these lines of Geraldine's weariness for the matter to be overlooked: see lines 72 - 74; 77; 92; 94; 102 - 104.

There is reason to think that Coleridge intended Geraldine's transformation from an evil creature to a redeemed one in the later parts of the poem that were never written. Ernest Hartley Coleridge more or less affirms Coleridge's intent to write the poem about Christabel's vicarious atonement for Geraldine's sins. There are the facts of Christabel's name to support this possible development. Christ's vicarious atonement for the redemption of sinful humanity is at the heart of Christian doctrine. There is also the representation of Christabel as a white dove in the poem, giving reminders of the whiteness of the sacrificial Lamb, Christ. The dove is bound by a snake, suggesting, of course, the form taken by Satan when in Eden he tempted the parents of mankind to their first sin.

With regard to the raw materials of the poem, we should be observant of Coleridge's treatment of vampire lore. He has refined and sophisticated the material from the crudeness that is often characteristic of such legend. In Geraldine we do not have the species of vampire that haunts the screen of fifth-rate horror films. Coleridge uses vampire lore but only as a basis for a profound and artistic study of the ambivalent character of both good and evil.

PART I, LINES 104 - 174

These seventy lines move the action of the poem from the forest where Christabel has found Geraldine to Christabel's chamber in the castle of her father, Sir Leoline. Christabel trusts Geraldine and believingly accepts her story of distress and fatigue (lines 104 - 111). She answers Geraldine's request and extends her hand in support. She welcomes Geraldine to her home and to the care and keep of Sir Leoline's household: "O well, bright dame! may you command / The service of Sir Leoline. . . ." (lines 106 & 107). Christabel promises that her father will bring his resources to Geraldine's aid and see that she returns safely to her home. Christabel leads Geraldine toward the castle, but they can only move slowly because of Geraldine's condition (line

112ff.). Christabel reveals to Geraldine that "Sir Leoline is weak in health," and that they must proceed through the castle quietly. Christabel invites Geraldine to share her bed (lines 121 & 122).

Christabel leads Geraldine across the moat that surrounds the castle, and through a little door in the middle of the castle gate (lines 123 - 128), the gate that is so constructed as to protect the castle from conquest. Perhaps Coleridge here intends a contrast between the iron defenses of the castle and Christabel's innocent trustingness. Line 129 reveals another sign of Geraldine's evil: she sinks at the threshold of the castle gate. She cannot go on without another physical contact with Christabel. Christabel must lift her up and carry her over the threshold (lines 130 - 134). The narrative suggests that the two ladies have escaped danger and fear (lines 135 & 136), but then, of course, the reader knows better. As they cross the court, Christabel devoutly asks her guest to join her in prayer to the Virgin, a prayer of thanksgiving for Geraldine's deliverance (lines 137 - 140). Geraldine cannot pray because of her evil, and she excuses her silence by claiming weariness.

Another portent of Geraldine's evil nature comes as they pass the kennel of "the mastiff old." The dog does not wake up, but, more tellingly, makes an angry moan in her sleep (lines 145 - 149). More revealing yet is the fact that she had never before moaned angrily in Christabel's presence. The narrator speculates that it is the scritching of the owl that does it, forcing the reader, therefore, to argue with him, to contradict him. Coleridge again uses the narrator to keep the reader involved in the story.

The third revealing sign of Geraldine's evil nature is the flashing up of fire as the two pass the hearth. The coals in the fireplace are dying; the woods is burned out, and there are only white ashes left. But when Geraldine walks by the fireplace, "A tongue of light, a fit of flame" spurts up (lines 154 - 159). Christabel does not know what is happening here, for she sees, besides the shield of Sir Leoline "in a murky old niche in the wall," only Geraldine's eye (lines 160 - 163). Christabel asks Geraldine to walk quietly because Sir Leoline is a light sleeper, and in his failing health his rest is precious. Christabel removes her sandals before they mount the stairs. They come at last to Christabel's chamber (lines 166 -174).

Comment

In these seventy lines there are four revelations of Geraldine's true character: (1) she sinks down at the threshold of the cast gate and cannot go on without Christabel's assistance, (2) she does not pray to the Virgin (3) the mastiff bitch growls in her sleep at Geraldine's presence within the castle walls, (4) the fire kindles when Geraldine passes the hearth. These events recall the tradition that an evil being could not enter a dwelling that had not had a Christian blessing bestowed upon it, except when there was some kind of human assistance extended, and further the traditional weakness of evil creatures in the presence of anything divine. These were standard medieval beliefs. There are additional examples of Geraldine's evil in the presence of the good in the further developments of the poem.

    Coleridge strengthens the medieval atmosphere of "Christabel" through continuing references to the castle, its surroundings and its furnishings. In line 108 he makes mention of Sir Leoline's "stout chivalry," in line 123 he mentions the moat around the castle, in line 125ff. he describes the defenses of the walls and gate, in line 128 he uses very nearly as **metaphor** a reference to an army having marched out through the castle gate, and in lines 162 & 163 he calls attention to Sir Leoline's shield and to the place of it "in a murky old niche in the wall." There are, of course, the continuing religious elements, here in line 139 the suggested prayer to the Virgin Mary.

The use of various kinds of shades and light throughout the poem should not be missed. The courtyard is steeped in moonlight, there is the momentary flaring of the flame in the fireplace, there is the murky shadow along the walls and in the hallway, and Christabel and Geraldine walk through glimmer and gloom.

The reader's involvement in the story is strengthened by the technique of the narrator's confiding truths to him about what is happening that Christabel does not know. One may be reminded of the tragedy that falls around Oedipus as the audience watching knows what he does not. On this subject we may note again the kind of rhetorical questions the narrator asks; here in line 149, "And what can ail the mastiff bitch?"; again in line 153, "For what can ail the mastiff bitch?" The narrator draws the reader into the story by not giving answers to the questions he asks.

That Christabel sees only Geraldine's eye when they pass by the fire fueled by Geraldine's evil nature may be the first incident of Christabel's entrancement: "And Christabel saw the lady's eye, / And nothing else saw she thereby. . . ." (lines 160 & 161) Though the spell is worked over Chritabel by the touch of Geraldine's deformed bosom, there are many instances in the poem where there is potent sorcery in the eye. If this is the initial bewitchment that Christabel suffers, her later passivity to Geraldine's suggestions is, of course, more easily understandable.

PART I, LINES 175 - 189

These lines provide more atmosphere in the poem, particularly again through Coleridge's different light effects. Christabel has brought Geraldine into her chamber, "The chamber carved so curiously. . . ." The room is dim but not so dim that its strange and sweet carvings cannot be seen. The craftsman designed it and constructed it particularly for a lady. One of its most charming features, and one that provides another element of religious setting in the poem, is an angel carved on the wall with a lamp by a "twofold silver chain" attached to its feet. Christabel trims the lamp, which was burning dimly, and as the light grows stronger, Geraldine sinks down upon the floor.

Comment

With respect to Coleridge's use of light in these lines, he tells that no moonlight enters the chamber (lines 175 & 176), but by his mention of it, moonlight enters the reader's mind and necessarily becomes, though actually absent, a part of the setting. It is a clever technique. Besides the introduction of moonlight through the denial of it, there is dimness in Christabel's chamber, a lamp burning "dead and dim," then a bright lamp left "swinging to and fro." Another of the betrayals of Geraldine's evil nature comes when in the brightness of the trimmed light she sinks onto the floor, partly because of the light, partly because of the benign presence of a Christian figure on the wall, the carven angel.

PART I, LINES 190 - 225

Christabel observes that Geraldine has sunk to the floor and, of course, thinks that her slump is because of her fatigue. For her refreshment she offers Geraldine some wine that her mother had made of wild flowers (lines 190 - 194). Continuing her trickery, Geraldine asks Christabel if Christabel's mother would pity so forlorn a maiden as she, exiled from her home because of capture by a gang of unknown men. Christabel discloses to Geraldine that her mother died in childbirth and tells of the story that her mother prophesied on her death-bed, how at Christabel's marriage she would hear the castle bell strike twelve (lines 197 - 201). Christabel wishes with a sense of urgency that her mother were present; Geraldine wishes with obvious fraud for the same.

Geraldine's voice suddenly alters, and she utters a curse, a curse toward the guardian spirit of Christabel's mother (lines 205 - 206). As she banishes the benign spirit, she declares her command of the hour and her possession of Christabel (lines 211 - 213). Again Christabel takes Geraldine's peculiar behavior to be the result of her weariness, she kneels by her side with eyes turned heavenward and says,

Alas! . . . this ghastly ride - Dear lady! it hath wildered you! The lady wiped her moist cold brow, And faintly said, ` 'tis over now!' (lines 216 - 219)

After expelling the guardian spirit and drinking another draft of the wild-flower wine, Geraldine rises from the floor, appearing to Christabel again as "the lofty lady" she found in the forest: "She was most beautiful to see,/ Like a lady of a far countree." (lines 226 & 227).

Comment

There is again in these lines the narrative technique of questions asked and left unanswered. The narrator asks about Geraldine, and the reader already knows that the answer is affirmative, "Can she the bodiless dead espy?" (line 209).

Any gift that Christabel offered would be virtuous, as are the powers of the wild-flower wine, and Geraldine may be restored by the drinking of it. But it is probably more true that she rises from the floor not primarily because she drinks the wine of virtuous powers, but, rather, because she has asserted her demonic powers over the guardian spirit of Christabel's mother and triumphed. It is obvious that Christabel has brought into her bedchamber a preternatural creature who possesses strange and potent power. Geraldine to this point remains unchanged in her character despite her contact with virtue.

Frequent references to the eye occur in "Christabel." The reader should observe the way the magical in the poem often finds expression in the power of the eye. Coleridge is refining for his own purpose one of those stock poetic devices of the 18th century. Geraldine stares "with unsettled eye" (line 208) at the spirit of Christabel's mother, and after she has asserted her power, "Her fair large eyes 'gan glitter bright...." (line 221).

PART I, LINES 226 - 278

The final stage of Geraldine's seduction of Christabel is described in the remaining fifty-two lines of Part I. She begins the most obvious physical aspects of the seduction in a way not surprising for a demonic creature in disguise: she makes reference to the way heavenly beings love Christabel and the way Christabel loves them (lines 226 - 229). Evil masquerading as good is, of course, one of the most prominent **themes** in literature. After she gives Christabel directions to disrobe and go to bed, she furthers her disguise by saying that she must pray before she sleeps (line 234).

Christabel obeys Geraldine's directions, disrobes, and "lay down in her loveliness." (lines 234 -238) But Christabel's mind is so disturbed that she cannot sleep, and in her distress she raises herself on her elbow and watches Geraldine undress (lines 239 - 244).

Slowly rolling her eyes around, Geraldine bows beneath the lamp, draws in her breath like a shudder, and her clothes rustle to the floor (lines 245 - 251). This is no doubt intended to be the most shocking, the most terrifying scene in the poem. When Geraldine's robe and vest fall off her to the floor, Christabel sees her deformed bosom and half her side. Coleridge's characterization is not at this point taken into too many specific details; he leaves it to the reader's imagination to fill in the exact configuration of this "sight to dream of, not to tell!" (lines 251 - 254) Geraldine looks stricken, she eyes Christabel, delays for a moment, then suddenly as if in defiance, "Collects herself in scorn and pride, / And lay down by the Maiden's side! - "(lines 255 - 262.)

Now comes the working of the spell over Christabel. Geraldine takes Christabel in her arms and with the touch of her bosom binds Christabel in the curse of her "shame" and "sorrow." Lines 267 - 278 contain the words of Geraldine's spell. She tells that Christabel will know her shame and sorrow that night and into the next day, but that she will not be able to tell anything of what has happened to her, only

'That in the dim forest Thou heard'st a low moaning, And found'st a bright lady, surpassing fair; And didst bring her home with thee in love and in charity, To shield her and shelter her from the damp air.' (lines 274 - 278)

Comment

The ambivalence of Geraldine's character, though she is, of course, predominantly evil, is evident in the scene of the spellbinding of Christabel. This ambivalence is first suggested when Geraldine says in connection with her reference to the mutual love that exists between Christabel and heavenly beings, "Even I in my degree will try / Fair maiden to requite you well." (lines 231 & 232). As "The Conclusion to Part II" tells us, and there are numerous evidences of the same thing in larger domains of his work, Coleridge was profoundly concerned with the constitution of man's inner self, his psyche (as we would be prone in our psychologizing time to say), his good motives and evil acts, his evil motives and good acts, the whole complex of man's mysterious self with its irrationality, its uncontrollableness, its caprice, its inseparable mixture of light and dark, its precarious place in the universe.

Geraldine for all her evil is not absolutely evil. There is even the suggestion that had she her way about herself, she would not seduce Christabel. Before she takes Christabel in her arms, she has a stricken look, and she seems from deep within herself to try to lift the burden of evil intent from her own heart (lines 256 - 258). There is the conspicuous delay in her seduction of Christabel (line 259). She even pronounces the curse with "doleful look" (line 265).

No less significant is Christabel's ambiguous feelings toward Geraldine. When she should have been going to sleep, she was propped up in bed watching Geraldine undress, hardly what one would expect of a maiden so pure. Christabel is obviously fascinated with Geraldine, and Coleridge no doubt intended the fascination to be partially sexual. It may be that for all her purity Christabel in part wants to be seduced. Purity in the human heart is never absolutely pure. The best of motives have their darker dimensions: the best of acts are never without something of destructive intent. The offer to help someone is so often a demand on that person's resources: the claim to be interested is so often a requirement to be found interesting. So often what lies beneath the claim of friendship is the compelling need of one person to use the other for the working out of his own psychic dilemmas. Coleridge of all people would be interested in the eternal presences of the grays. Christabel's ambiguity is only slightly less apparent in the seduction scene than Geraldine's. Christabel's interest in Geraldine's disrobing of herself is congruent with the sexual meanings conspicuous in the whole of the working of the curse. There is, of course, in the background of the encounter the mass of legend concerning the sexual mystery of vampires, lamias, witches, and other such preternatural beings.

From line 160, as noted earlier, it may be that Christabel has come to some degree under Geraldine's influence. The extent of her enslavement is not known until the juncture in the poem of the curse, but it is difficult to pass over so obvious a development as that of Geraldine, the guest, ordering Christabel, the host, to disrobe and go to bed. From about line 226, Geraldine seems to take over the relationship. There is the further evidence of Christabel's disturbed state of mind before the seduction in bed: see lines 293ff.

LINES 279 - 331, "THE CONCLUSION TO PART I"

This section of the poem describes Christabel's restless sleep after Geraldine's pronouncement of the curse. The Conclusion asks if this Christabel, now "With open eyes (ah woe is me!) / Asleep, and dreaming fearfully," can really be the lovely, trusting, peaceful Christabel who was seen praying by the oak tree, "Kneeling in the moonlight, / To make her gentle vows...." (lines 279 - 297) Christabel's disturbance of soul is as profound as is Geraldine's calm. The "Conclusion" draws the contrast in their spiritual states. While Christabel sleeps with open eyes and fearful dreams (lines 292 - 296), Geraldine as she holds Christabel in her arms slumbers "still and mild." Good in the presence of evil is distraught: evil in the presence of good is unchanged.

Lines 302 - 310 tell of the sympathy of nature with the curse. The involvement of the whole of the created order with sin is a familiar Biblical statement. The Yahwist writer in the early chapters of Genesis speaks of the way in which man's sin corrupted nature, that nature fell when man fell. The Apostle Paul tells that the universe, not just man, waits for deliverance from the curse of sin. John Donne and John Milton presuppose or articulate the concept of nature sharing in man's sin. Here in "Christabel" during the spellbinding sorcery of Geraldine, the night-birds are quiet.

Lines 311 - 318 speak of Christabel in the terms of innocent childhood. Though she is in the evil embrace of Geraldine, "she seems to smile / As infants at a sudden light!" Christabel's essential goodness is unchanged. Though she is in a wilderness, she remains beautiful (lines 319 - 321), and her established inclination to the good continues, even while she sleeps: "Like a youthful hermitess, / Beauteous in a wilderness, / Who praying always, prays in sleep." (lines 320 - 322) She can in the presence of evil have "a vision sweet" and sustain her faith.

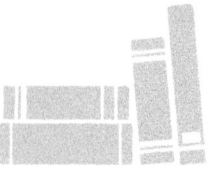

CHRISTABEL

TEXTUAL ANALYSIS

PART II

PART II, LINES 332 - 359

The first twenty-seven lines of Part II are concerned with the practice at Sir Leoline's castle, Langdale hall, of ringing the matin bell as a warning bell to every soul "From Bratha Head to Wyndermere." Since the time of the death of Christabel's mother, the Baron has had the sacristan pause between each strike of the matinal bell and tell forty-five beads. The ringing of the bell is intended to be a reminder to the living of their mortality. The practice is, of course, opposite to the usual service of Morning Prayer that begins the new life of a new day. Perhaps Sir Leoline's practice of having the matin bell rung as a warning, rather than as a thanksgiving, rung to knell its hearers "back to a world of death," is intended to reinforce the general atmosphere of death that pervades the poem. This use of the matin bell would be in keeping with the dead and decaying condition of the forest in which Christabel finds Geraldine.

Bracy the bard, who will be sent by Sir Leoline to Roland de Vaux later in the poem, tells of the echo that is made by three sinful ghosts at each pealing of the bell (lines 350 - 355). The sacristan's ringing of the bell for the purpose of reminding the people of their sinfulness is echoed with a reply from the ghosts, called in line 355 a "death-note." Their reply seems to be a mockery of the hope of the living. They mock the sacristan's prayers for salvation from sin with the affirmation that there is no salvation, only death as the inevitable end of all things. If the matin bell and the rosary are intended to remind the living of Christ's sacrificial death for man's sin, the ghosts reply that Christ's death was only a death and had no efficacy for sinners. The devil is there also, the incarnation of evil, the actual personalized force of sin in the world, the principal agent of sin and death - his purpose is further to distort and mock the good: "Just as their [the ghosts'] one! two! three! is ended, / The devil mocks the doleful tale/with a merry peal from Borodale." (lines 357 - 359).

Comment

Distortion of the good by the evil is the most evident **theme** in the twenty-seven lines at the beginning of Part II. The goodness of life has been distorted first of all by the death of Christabel's mother at a time that should be one of the most joyful occasions for human beings, the birth of a child. There is the resulting death in life of Sir Leoline, distorting the goodness of each new day with a stubborn fixation on death. There is the distortion of the bell, intended to sound the gladness of worship and praise, first by wrong use (squandering the gifts of life), and then by evil intent of the ghosts in Langdale Pike and Witch's Lair. Finally, there is the mockery of the devil,

The **theme** of the distortion of the good by the evil follows in a natural and consistent way the violation of Christabel's essential goodness by Geraldine's essential evil. Following this line of interpretation, there is a contrast between the developments in these beginning lines of Part II and the last three lines of "The Conclusion to Part I." Those three lines contain a moral tag, not greatly unlike that at the end of "The Ancient Mariner," affirming "That saints will aid if men will call...."

It states in the midst of Christabel's corruption the blessing of Providential care for those who will but remember to ask. But Christabel has been remembering and asking! It may be that the affirmation of the love of God at the end of the "Conclusion" is intended further to delineate the absence of that love in Geraldine's seduction of Christabel and in the world of death of Sir Leoline's castle.

There have been various uses of an echo technique throughout the poem. There was the echo of the cock to the owls, the mastiff bitch to the clock, Geraldine's moaning to Christabel's silent prayer, the reader's answers to the narrator's questions - now all the sounds that mock the matin bell. If one considers "Christabel" to be a story about good and evil, their inner workings and outward expressions, one may find in the echo technique a supporting literary structure for the way in which good is ambiguously echoed by evil (Christabel's charity to Geraldine is "echoed" by Geraldine's corruption of Christabel), and evil is ambiguously echoed by good (considering particularly the possibility that Sir Leoline and Roland de Vaux were to be restored through the evil agency of Geraldine's shame and sorrow).

PART II, LINES 360 - 392

These lines will advance the story to the point that Geraldine meets Sir Leoline.

Apparently Geraldine is awakened from her sleep with Christabel in her arms by the devil's "merry peal from Borodale." It is no doubt significant that the peal comes "through mist and cloud." (lines 360 - 363). After recovering herself from her own natural dread of what she is, after overcoming the persistent tendency to become overwhelmed by her own evil, Geraldine "rises lightly from the bed. . . ." (lines 362 - 363). She dresses herself in garments that represent purity, "silken vestments white," and awakens Christabel, never doubting Christabel's enslavement to her will. Notice also that the purity of Geraldine's garments is not the only aspect of her appearance to which Coleridge calls attention. The manner in which she dresses her hair forms a deliberate contrast to the quality of the clothes. In the line immediately following the description of her "vestments," Coleridge has it that Geraldine "tricks her hair in lovely plight. . . ." (line 365) The poetic effect of the word tricks is obvious; plight has its roots in the Anglo -Saxon and Middle English plight, meaning in the older language risk and danger, and having in the later language danger also as one of its principal meanings.

When Christabel awakes she finds Geraldine fairer for having slept: ". . . fairer yet! [than she had been when Christabel first found her] and yet more fair! / For she belike hath drunken deep / Of all the blessedness of sleep!" (lines 374 - 376) Geraldine gives the appearance of being thankful for her rest and recovery (lines 377 - 380). But goodness is only in the eye of the beholder; Christabel sees what is in keeping with her usual trusting attitude toward the world. The parenthesis in line 379 helps to identify Geraldine's fraud. Christabel awakens with an oppressive sense of guilt, falters in her speech because of her great confusion, but without losing her natural sweetness of temperament greets Geraldine with great "perplexity of mind." (lines 381 - 386). Christabel rises quickly from bed, dresses herself quickly, and, after praying, probably also quickly leads Geraldine forth from her bedchamber to meet her father, Sir Leoline.

Comment

There is a consistent stillness in the universe of "Christabel." Movement takes place among the characters, but the creaturely movement is surrounded by natural death. The atmospheric effects of the poem at the beginning of the lines explicated above are the same as those in the forest when Christabel found Geraldine on the other side of the oak tree.

Lines 374 - 376 describe Geraldine's enhanced loveliness in the morning to be the result of deep sleep. But there may be also the suggestion that she is restored because she has drunk deeply of Christabel's goodness.

Despite the curse she is under, Christabel retains the ability to pray. She does not understand the cause of her sense of sin, but her faculties are not entirely taken over by Christabel. Of course, Geraldine's curse had contained nothing about the obliteration of Christabel's religious devotion, although it may seem strange in a way that Christabel would still have this ability to pray. Christabel's prayer "That He, who on the cross did groan, / Might wash away her sins unknown" (lines 389 - 390) expresses what was often a dilemma in Coleridge's own personal life, a dilemma that he spoke of frequently in his notebooks and not infrequently in his letters, misery from "sins unknown."

PART II, LINES 393 - 402)

Sir Leoline meets Geraldine in his presence-room. He embraces Christabel and then greets Geraldine "With cheerful wonder in his eyes. . . ." The Baron welcomes Christabel's guest in a way that seems appropriate for such a lady.

Comment

Coleridge has made mention before of Geraldine's stature. He speaks early in the poem of her "stately neck," and again in line 226 of "the lofty lady." He seems to intend a contrast between the different appearances of Christabel and Geraldine with regard to size. At line 393 he speaks of the two as "The lovely maid and the lady tall. . . ." He had in "The Conclusion to Part I" said that as Christabel and Geraldine slept together that Geraldine seemed to be a mother with her child. The difference in the appearance of the two might reinforce the impression of innocence in the presence of evil. As Geraldine meets Sir Leoline attention is focused again on her brightness: ". . . such welcome . . . / As might beseem so bright a dame!" (lines 401 & 402).

PART II, LINES 403 - 426

Geraldine tells to Sir Leoline her story and in the process identifies herself as the daughter of Lord Roland de Vaux of Tryermaine. Sir Leoline grows pale when he hears Lord Roland's name (lines 403-407). The narrator explains Sir Leoline's reaction: Sir Leoline and Lord Roland had been friends in their youth, but they quarreled, apparently because of rumor (line 409), insulted each other (lines 461 & 417), and parted "ne'er to meet again!" Since that time they have both retained their haughty silence, but neither had been able to overcome the inward scars that were made by their separation (lines 421-426). Neither had been able to find a friend like the other had been to him (lines 419 & 420).

Comment

The **simile** Coleridge uses to describe the broken friendship between the two lords gives cause for further speculation about the character and condition of Geraldine. The **simile** in question comes in lines 421-423: "They stood aloof, the scars remaining, / Like cliffs which had been rent asunder; / A dreary sea now flows between...."

Geraldine is possibly meant to be the child of the broken love between the two men. The scars of their alienation have possibly become transferred to Geraldine. She displays on her bosom "The marks of that which once hath been." In one sense her aggression toward Christabel is therefore an expression of the disposition of evil to beget itself. But in a larger sense it may be the yearning of evil for redemption, as sadism is at heart really a yearning for deeper relationship yet undiscovered.

Lines 410-413 contain to this point in the poem Coleridge's most pointed statement on the subject of mortal weakness. They suggest also the inextricable mixture of love and hate in the human heart.

PART II, LINES 427 - 446

Sir Leoline remembers his deep love for Lord Roland as he looks into Geraldine's face (strange that good can be seen in evil places, even though the evil compounds itself into worse evil by fraudulently presenting itself as good), and he is passionately moved in his heart at the memory (lines 427 - 430). He makes an oath that he will declare Geraldine's kidnappers to be "base as spotted infamy!" (lines 431 - 437) He will open his tourney court to them that they may come and deny his charge (lines 438 - 441). He will welcome the opportunity of ridding the world of such evil as they embody (lines 441 - 443). As he speaks, "his eye in lightning rolls!"

Comment

Sir Leoline not only forgets his age, but he seems also conveniently to have repressed his own evil when he makes the powerful denunciation of Geraldine's abductors. The narrator has just told of Sir Leoline's and Lord Roland's shattered friendship, owing to the human frailty of others and to the human frailty of themselves, and then Sir Leoline asserts his vindictive fury toward those men with reptile souls who stole away Geraldine from her home. Were he to begin his extermination program in the most obvious place, dislodging "reptile soul / From the bodies and forms of men," he would no doubt first exterminate himself. Sir Leoline obviously participates in that original sin of man, symbolized Biblically by the serpent that brings about man's fall. He is not only a participant in the origin of a sinful act, the break of a love relationship with another human being, but he seeks to place the blame for evil on to other men, men with "reptile souls." One of the first evidences of human sin in the Garden of Eden story (intended mythologically to portray the origin and consequence of human sin) is that both Adam and Eve try to place the blame for what has happened outside themselves. Although it is a long way from Jerusalem to Athens, although hubris is not exactly the same as hamartia, Oedipus consistently does the same - fails to see his own nature in the fury of his blame of others. Besides all of this, Sir Leoline shares in the nature of sinful Man in his incapacity to distinguish good from evil; he misses entirely the demonism of the glittering lady before him.

We have noted before Coleridge's frequent reference to the eye. Sir Leoline has an eye that "in lightning rolls" as he makes his proclamation. Eighteenth-century poetry had numerous flashing eyes. Coleridge shows a predisposition to take over and use such exclamations that suggest unlimited power. Geraldine's power is an example of Coleridge's intense interest in energy that has been misdirected into violent, even rebellious, expression. Sir Leoline's power is to an extent the same, although there is an obvious impotence in his character as well.

PART II, LINES 447 - 474

Sir Leoline is susceptible to Geraldine's entrancement, and she must entrance him if she is to retain her hold on Christabel. He must be bound under her spell, or he will be suspicious and maybe defeating of her purposes.

With tears on his face from the remembrance of his love for Lord Roland, and out of sympathy with Geraldine's plight, he embraces Geraldine, and Geraldine prolongs the embrace in the joy of triumph at having made him her victim (lines 446 - 450). Christabel, knowing the deeper meanings of what is happening, "shrunk and shuddered" at the sight of Geraldine in her father's embrace: ". . . a vision fell / Upon the soul of Christabel, / The vision of fear, the touch and pain!" (lines 451 - 453) When Christabel remembers the touch of Geraldine's bosom, she draws "in her breath with a hissing sound. . . ." (lines 458 & 459).

Sir Leoline turns around toward Christabel, startled at what he hears. But, he sees only Christabel in prayer, with smiles on her lips and in her eyes (lines 461 - 469). Her expression has suddenly returned to what it was when the first trance of the curse had passed, before she slept in Geraldine's arms. (cf. lines 311 - 331). He asks Christabel what disturbs her, but, of course, being under Geraldine's spell she can reveal nothing.

Comment

Sir Leoline, for all his exhibitions of power in the poem, does not in the final analysis seem a particularly strong character. His susceptibility is one of his most conspicuous traits. He may be because of his weaknesses the most human of the four characters in the poem. Christabel's reaction to Sir Leoline's embrace of Geraldine reveals that she is taking unto herself as time passes something of Geraldine's essential evil. Geraldine is all the time becoming more beautiful and more seductively feminine.

PART II, LINES 475 - 518

Geraldine's invasion tactics for Sir Leoline next assume the form of a feigned concern for Christabel's feelings. She blends "sorrow" and "grace" in her expression of alarm over the possibility of having offended Christabel; her seeming compassion makes her appear even move divine (lines 475 - 479). She brings the Baron even more completely under her influence through the strategic maneuver of asking that she might be sent home right away to her father's mansion.

Of course, Sir Leoline will have nothing of the sort, just as Geraldine knew. Rather, he gives what amounts in the poem to thirty-five lines of directions to Bracy the bard for going to Tryermaine with news of Geraldine's safety. Bard Bracy will go, orders Sir Leoline, "with music sweet and loud," and will in proud array (lines 485 - 488) hasten to Roland de Vaux. Bracy must dress himself and his understudy in solemn attire to ensure a speedy journey. Sir Leoline orders Bracy to deliver to Lord Roland the news (1) that his daughter is safe at Langdale hall (lines 502 & 503), (2) that Lord Roland is to come with his hosts to meet Sir Leoline and to take Geraldine home (lines 505 - 507), and (3) that Sir Leoline wishes to speak to Lord Roland his repentance for the "words of fierce disdain" that he spoke in their youth (lines 511 -518).

Comment

Geraldine steadily gains in Sir Leoline's confidence and affection to the end of the poem. It is for one thing because of her personal attractiveness, but it is also because of the new emotional vulnerability Sir Leoline feels in his poignant memory of Lord Roland and his keen regret at their abandoned relationship. From the point of Geraldine's prolonged embrace of Sir Leoline, Christabel will steadily lose her father's favor.

Of course, Bracy being a poet would deliver any news he had to give "with music sweet and loud." Comment has been made elsewhere in this study of Coleridge's continual associations of poetry with music, the most famous of which is in "Kubla Khan," where the young poet with "flashing eyes" and "floating hair" would build the pleasure-dome "with music loud and long." Such music is assigned to Bracy the bard in lines 485, 499 & 500, and 501. Loud music is to be named again in the ensuing lines.

PART II, LINES 519 - 563

These forty-four lines contain Bracy's account to Sir Leoline of the dream he has had in which he saw Christabel in the form of a dove "... uttering fearful moan, / Among the green herbs in the forest alone." (lines 535 & 536). Bracy tells that in his strange dream he could not at first see why the dove struggled on "the grass and green herbs underneath the old tree." (line 540). But when he went closer "To search out what might there be found; / And what the sweet bird's trouble meant" (lines 541 - 544), he found the dove bound around the wings and neck be a bright green snake (lines 549 - 554). He relates how the snake had its head placed by the dove's head and moved in a kind of unison with the bird (lines 552 -554). He awoke from the dream at this point, he says, and found it to be the midnight hour (lines 555 -556). He tells Sir Leoline that the dream has remained vivid in his mind, and that he has vowed subsequently to go into the forest and "With music strong and saintly song" rid the forest of any unholy thing that might be there (line 561).

Bracy tells his dream to Sir Leoline by way of asking the boon that he might be permitted to delay his journey to Lord Roland long enough to go and purify the forest of the unblest thing of which he had been warned in his dream (lines 523 - 530).

Comment

The dove that serves in Bracy's dream as a symbol of Christabel is apparently a pet dove that Sir Leoline keeps in the castle and calls "Christabel." Bracy's dream, of course, is a paradigm of Christabel's being bound by Geraldine. In the dream the dove flutters on "the grass and the green herbs underneath the old tree" where Christabel went to pray and where she found Geraldine. Bracy wakes from his dream just at the hour when Christabel goes into the wood. The splendid detail of the dream with regard to the way the snake moves in unison with the dove recalls (in the time sequence of the dream anticipates) Geraldine's embrace of Christabel while they slept together. The snake has imprisoned the dove by coiling around it; Geraldine's embrace had been called Christabel's prison (cf. lines 303 & 304).

Again it is with that special kind of power that one can only assume is imaginative power, poetic power, creative power that Bracy says he will purify the forest. The **metaphor** of music identifies the kind of power that is Bracy's. The relationships that Coleridge makes between poetry and music are discussed at some length in the commentary on "Kubla Khan."

PART II, LINES 564 - 620

Sir Leoline has been only "half-listening" to Bracy the bard and seems to take the dream as only another piece of entertainment from the poet. Sir Leoline has "heard him with a smile. . . ." (line 565). His natural obtuseness combined with the further reduction of whatever awareness he has by Geraldine's hold over him is enough to make him miss the point of Bracy's dream.

He has heard him well enough, however, to know the framework of the story, for he takes the barest outline of what Bracy has said and uses it as a vehicle for promising Geraldine that he and her father will crush the evil that has kept them separated from one another through the years. In the Baron's adaptation of Bracy's dream for **metaphor**, Geraldine becomes the dove, the alienation between the two friends the snake.

Of course Geraldine is pleased with Sir Leoline's casual attitude toward Bracy's dream. Her conquest of him is evident in his continuing attitude of "wonder and love" toward her, in his adaptation of Bracy's dream in her behalf, and in his kissing her on the forehead as a seal to his promise (lines 567 -572). Geraldine continues the disguise of the wronged maiden as she looks with "large bright eyes" shyly to the floor after Sir Leoline kisses her, as she blushes modestly, as she turns in explicit courtesy from Sir Leoline, and softly gathers up her train (lines 573 - 578). She then expresses her triumph by looking sideways at Christabel and reversing threateningly her eyes into the eyes of a snake (lines 579 - 581). The narrator interjects a prayer to the Virgin for Christabel's protection.

Lines 583 - 588 further describe Geraldine's serpentine expression. Christabel is stunned by the expression, experiencing in it the full horror of what has happened to her, realizing with a renewed terror the extent of the ugly coil that Geraldine has bound her with. In this new shock of recognition she is first "in dizzy trance," then she stumbles and shudders aloud, expressing her humiliation and fear in the means one would expect of Geraldine, "with a hissing sound. . . ." (lines 589 - 591). Geraldine naturally hides her serpentine look from Sir Leoline and avoids any trace of responsibility for Christabel's behavior by turning round and rolling "her large bright eyes divine / Wildly on Sir Leoline." (lines 595 & 596).

The first marked moment of Christabel's earning her father's disfavor begins when she imitates Geraldine's "look of dull and treacherous hate" in full view of Sir Leoline. Lines 597 - 612 describe Christabel's trance. The impact of Geraldine's expression when she "looked askance" at Christabel had gone so deep in her that Christabel could see nothing else (line 598). Coleridge describes the depth of the penetration of Geraldine's evil look by saying that she had drunken in the image of Geraldine's "shrunken serpent eyes" (lines 601 - 604) The method of it was "forced unconsciously sympathy." (line 609).

With the passing of these moments of utter immobility and prostration before Geraldine's demonic expression, Christabel pauses and prays, and then recovering something of her usual strength, falls down at her father's feet and begs him to send Geraldine away. Being still under Geraldine's influence, she can give no explanation for her entreaty.

Comment

Having been invaded and infected by Geraldine's witchcraft, Sir Leoline is unable to know the truth of what is happening to him and to his daughter. The touch of Geraldine's bosom has helped render him insensitive to Bracy's warning. But there is in his character, as suggested earlier, a kind of predisposition that makes him easy prey to Geraldine's attack. He had helped to make himself impotent through an inordinate involvement with the memory of his dead wife. He is the old man of failing health, given to a kind of maudlin enjoyment of his personal misfortunes and incapacities and those of the universe. He has given up any kind of productive encounter with the forces that be and has prematurely retreated into the secure chambers of senility. He seems to be enjoying bad health. He may summon up a noble rage and make loud proclamations about what he will do, but his weakness of character is never too far beneath the bombast. His self-centered sentimentality is in excess of the effects of Geraldine's curse - perhaps we should say it is present before Geraldine comes along.

Christabel's reaction to Geraldine's "look of dull and treacherous hate" recalls Geraldine's behavior as she prepared to work the spell over Christabel in the last lines of <u>Part I</u>. The terms of the narration are much the same. Compare

And drew in her breath with a hissing sound. (line 459)

Stumbling on the unsteady ground Shuddered aloud, with a hissing sound. (lines 590 & 591)

to

Then drawing in her breath aloud, Like one that shuddered, she unbound The cincture from beneath her breast. (lines (247 - 249)

Several other suggestions of Geraldine's ambiguous nature occur in this part of the poem. Her actions here seem contradictory in that she looks at Christabel ". . . with somewhat of malice, and more of dread. . . ." (line 586). It is unexpected that she would dread at all, being so resolute in her purpose. But she has experienced dread at another point in the poem; when the devil's merry mockery of the matin bell has awakened her, she "shakes off her dread" before she rises to dress herself after sleeping with Christabel (line 362). There is also in lines 592 - 594 the implication that Geraldine does not entirely want to be what she is. She vacillates between impulses benign and sinister. At the most basic level, this pattern is in keeping with the traditional behavior of vampires in the folklore about them. For all of their ugliness and evil intent, they are frequently presented as being deserving of pity. Stories about vampires often have them doing acts of malice and destruction that they do not want to do. They are victimized by some past sin, the evil effects of which they do not alone, left to their resources, have the power to expiate. Geraldine's character and behavior bear close resemblance to that of traditional vampires. Of the kinds of vampire creatures that exist in legend, Geraldine is most like the lamia because of its serpent characteristics. Coleridge would certainly be cognizant of the stories about these preternatural creatures, and, of course, as is particularly obvious in this part of the poem, Geraldine is a kind of serpent-woman. Geraldine's ambiguous nature would be harmonious with what is probably the major **theme** of the poem, the ambiguous intermixture of good in evil, of evil in good.

PART II, LINES 621 - 655

Sir Leoline with continuing blindness has interpreted Christabel's imitation of Geraldine's glance, particularly in conjunction with Christabel's plea that he send Geraldine away, as flagrant inhospitality, and he probably takes the inhospitality to be the result of jealousy on her part for the attention he is giving Geraldine.

From line 621 to line 635 the narrator addresses Sir Leoline (again expecting the reader to give the answer to the questions), relating Christabel's seeming misbehavior to her deceased mother's pains and hopes in her behalf. The narrator's questions and comments here serve to point out the nearly unique degree of Sir Leoline's rage toward his daughter. He is humiliated at Christabel's actions and feels his honor to defiled by her breach of all the principles of hospitality (lines 636 - 644). His humiliation is made all the worse because Christabel's inhospitality is being expressed toward the daughter of his old and beloved friend (line 645), and also because her actions are giving him too many acutely unpleasant reminders of his inhospitable behavior of years ago.

Sir Leoline turns to Bracy the bard and flings his anger in his face, displacing the rage that he feels toward his daughter in the more acceptable direction of the poet's disobedience. He scolds him for not having carried out his directions and orders him from the castle (line 648 - 652). Bracy leaves the room, and Sir Leoline, turning from his humiliated daughter with feelings of humiliation toward her, leads Geraldine forth.

Comment

In lines 621 and 622, and again in lines 634 and 635, the narrator asks two of those rhetorical questions that operate to involve the reader and propel the action forward. As he addresses Sir Leoline the reader finds himself giving his own answers to the questions. The reader tends to side with Christabel, of course, for Sir Leoline has missed the reason for her behavior because of his somewhat natural self-centeredness compounded with the effects of Geraldine's sorcery.

Perhaps the narrator's questions and comments in lines 621 - 635 show Sir Leoline's complex of feelings toward Christabel, his intense love for her and his unconfessed hatred for her because her birth meant his wife's death. This bold analysis of psychological interaction reflects Coleridge's characteristic interest in states of mind and currents of feeling in interfamilial relationships. Coleridge was typically unashamed in his analyses of himself (insofar, of course, as his own defenses would permit him to go) and in his analyses of his family members. He does a great deal of analysis in his notebooks of himself and of those close to him. His presentation in "Christabel" of the puzzling, unpredictable, incongruous household of the human heart, dwelling place of those strange bedfellows, love and hate, who find each other antithetical but indissoluble partners, is consistent with so many of the utterances he made to his private diaries about himself and those around him.

PART II, LINES 656 - 677, "THE CONCLUSION TO PART II"

This "Conclusion" does nothing narratively; it does not advance the action of the poem, and it does not comment on the events that have transpired in the way in which "The Conclusion to Part I" does. Most readers do not consider it a conclusion at all. The majority of critics feel that it has no function at all with regard to the outcome of the poem.

But "The Conclusion to Part II" has been the subject of much critical discussion. Some consider it conclusive in a much more encompassing sense than only in its relationship to Part II of the poem. One critic, Professor Edward E. Bostetter, says that "The Conclusion to Part II" is a sign that the poet had taken the poem as far as he could. But this needs some further explanation: Bostetter affirms that writing poetry was for Coleridge a process in which he was constantly exploring his inner self, that it was a means with which he tried to come to grips with the psychological and metaphysical problems that he confronted as a human being seeking a meaningful relationship to himself and to his world.

Bostetter says that the essential problem with "Christabel," the one essential reason the poem remained unfinished, was that Coleridge could find no answer to the questions the poem had raised, could not discover the **metaphysical** deftness of touch necessary to unravel the tangle of good and evil the poem had become, could not sufficiently exercise that inner power that brings order out of chaos - not just in the poem but in his own life.

However right or wrong Bostetter's interpretation is, and there is much to recommend it, there is every reason to accept what he says about poetry being for Coleridge an active personal involvement, even a kind of life - and - death struggle. It is a statement that would serve as a pretty substantial generalization for perhaps all of the major English Romantics. They were not poets who could live at much distance to their manuscripts. When William Wordsworth wrote *The Prelude*, he was in his own consciousness of himself and his task doing nothing less important than what Moses did on Mt. Sinai. *The Prelude* is a poem about William Wordsworth writing *The Prelude*. William Blake would liken the poet's imagination to Christ himself. Keats as man and poet wanted to live every moment as expressibly meaningful, wanted to live a life where every moment is an important as getting married. Every poem becomes the ceremonialization of a moment.

Lines 656 - 664 of "The Conclusion to Part II" expresses the preternatural loveliness of a child "Singing, dancing to itself...." The child is as much like a daffodil (thinking in Wordsworthian terms) as it could be; it is closer to the wellsprings of meaning, it is more intimately rooted in the Divine than man could ever be again. Coleridge is saying much the same thing here that

Wordsworth says about the child in the "Intimations Ode" and in much the same language. Compare lines 658 - 661 of "The Conclusion to Part II" of "Christabel" with lines 85 - 89 and lines 108 - 122 of Wordsworth's "Ode: Intimations of Immortality." But there are important differences in the larger treatment of the subject in Wordsworth's poem.

Here in "The Conclusion to Part II," the father is overcome with love for his child and to such an extent that he cannot find any longer the right words to gather up all of the ". . . pleasures [that] flow in so thick and fast / Upon his heart," and he finds himself expressing ". . . his love's excess / With words of unmeant bitterness." (lines 662 - 665) Coleridge had sent the lines of "The Conclusion to Part II" in a letter to Robert Southey on 6 May 1801. He commented to Southey about them, "A very **metaphysical** account of fathers calling their children rogues, rascals, and little varlets, etc."

From line 666 to the end, the "Conclusion" becomes increasingly complex in thought and increasingly somber in tone. Coleridge attempts to articulate some of the most subtle and some of the most inexpressible feelings of the human heart. Any attempt at paraphrase of the lines may be so clumsy as to damage the effect of the "Conclusion," however clumsy it might be in its own right. But Coleridge seems to be saying (1) (lines 666 & 667) that one feels a peculiar excitement in thinking of such opposite states as love and bitterness at one and the same time, (2) (lines 668 & 669) that there is a thrill in thinking of that which one knows is unpermitted, and (3) (lines 670 - 672) that one can feel more compassion for someone one loves if one can insult that person's humanness, that is, if one can add to another's weaknesses by calling attention to them, one can more freely and more greatly love that person. The "wild word" of line 671 is the word of insult, of humiliation, and so much more enables the insulter to love because he feels "A sweet recoil of... pity." (line 672) In reply to William Blake's **stanza** in "The Human Abstract,"

Pity would be no more If we did not make somebody poor; And mercy no more could be If all were as happy as we,

Coleridge would say, absolutely so - such is the nature of the beast called man.

Comment

One of the roots of this psychical necessity that "The Conclusion to Part II" reveals is that all of us live better with our mortality if we get everyone on our own level. Nothing is more humiliating than to find someone who seems to have discovered secrets about life and death that we do not possess. And so, if we find someone we greatly admire, and we know his gifts and achievements exceed ours, we seek to balance the scales by discovering the skeletons in his closets, the places under the rug of his psychological defenses where he has swept unmanageable dirt. We cannot tolerate such a person as a member of our own species unless he possesses at least some of the weaknesses that are ours, until we discover that he is also bound by the same limits of mortality that bind us. Perhaps this is the explanation of sadistic acts - the sadist essentially seeks a deep sense of belonging to the human community, and since he has failed at what he considers rising to its level, he will strike out and bring it down to his level. All of what we consider sexual aberrations may be explained in the same way, a passionate clutching after belonging, an intense yearning after the degree of respect for ourselves as creatures that our mortality and more-than-mortality requires. The use of socially unpermitted language in sexual relations that psychiatrists report their patients' feeling guilt about is much of what Coleridge is writing about in "The Conclusion to Part II," jealousy at feeling that the other person has come in contact with resources of beauty and power beyond that which has been permitted to us. The father who watches his child so joyous in its "Singing, dancing to itself" that it seems "A fairy thing with red round cheeks" is first of all jealous that the child "always finds, and never seeks," exactly what he, the parent, always seeks and never, or almost never, finds. The child has naturally, even carelessly, found a preternatural contact with the Absolute that is too often denied the father. The child possesses what the father cannot have, that "Singing, dancing" joy that exists only when the human creature has not yet been made aware of such things as sickness, and death. The child remains in intimate touch with the Eden of uncorrupted joy. The parent feels joy only occasionally, and then more in the "giddiness of heart and brain" that Milton describes as the drunkenness of Adam and Eve just after the fall. The parent lives "in a world of sin" (line 673) where joyous excitement is rarely caused by anything but rage and pain. The child that Coleridge describes "Singing, dancing" is the human creature before the Fall, the fairy creature before he has made decisions and found them more often wrong than right, more often leading to sorrow than leading to joy.

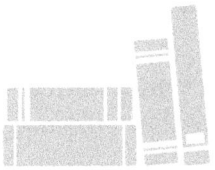

CHRISTABEL

ESSAY QUESTIONS AND ANSWERS

Question: Comment on the character of Geraldine.

Answer: With regard to Geraldine's appearance, the emphasis throughout the poem is on her external beauty. The introduction of Geraldine at the beginning of the poem, for example, calls attention to her brightness and glitter, but it is all of the external sort. The narrator from time to time calls attention to Geraldine's clothing; perhaps the concentration on these externals is intended to give an emphasis of contrast to the description of her deformed bosom and side, which in a variant reading are described as "lean and old and foul of hue." Still after Geraldine's deformity is revealed, the narrator speaks of her as "so bright a dame," "fair Geraldine," with "large bright eyes divine." Sir Leoline in meeting her "deemed her sure a thing divine." There is in the entrancement of others when meeting her the charm and the attractiveness of evil. In this sense "Christabel" is a re-enactment of so much of the content of Book II of Spenser's *The Faerie Queene*. Geraldine is most obviously an evil creature, of course, in her possession of supernatural powers. Besides being able to bind Christabel and Sir Leoline, Christabel's father, in a spell, she has the power to drive away the guardian spirit of Christabel's dead mother. Also she seems to be able to communicate with the dead.

Question: Give a summary of the story of "Christabel."

Answer: In Part I Christabel, daughter of Sir Leoline, goes out from the castle where she lives into the woods for the purpose of praying for her betrothed knight who is far away from her. The time is midnight, the time of the setting of many so-called Gothic stories. Christabel kneels beneath an old oak tree. She is soon startled by a moan from the other side of the tree under which she is praying. Upon going to the other side of the tree to investigate the sound she has heard, she discovers a strange and beautiful lady who says she is weak from fatigue, and who identifias herself as Geraldine. Geraldine tells her story to Christabel. She was abducted by five warriors whom she did not know. They brought her to this wood, placed her beneath the oak tree, and swore soon to return. Geraldine hears the castle bell of Langdale hall, the name of the castle where Christabel lives, and she asks Christabel's help in fleeing.

Christabel takes Geraldine to the castle, and this is the first we hear of Sir Leoline. Sir Leoline, says Christabel, will provide knightly protection for Geraldine and will ensure her escape from the warriors and a safe return to her home. Christabel leads Geraldine to her chamber in the castle. There she confides to Geraldine the fact that her mother died giving her birth, and that she has promised to hear the castle bell ring on Christabel's wedding day. Geraldine assumes a different disposition suddenly and drives the spirit of Christabel's mother away. She promises to repay Christabel's kindness to her. Christabel watches Geraldine undress with too great a fascination, they go to bed, Geraldine touches Christabel with her deformed bosom and then tells Christabel that she has worked a spell on her. "The

Conclusion to <u>Part I</u>" tells of Christabel's troubled sleep and dreams.

<u>Part II</u> begins the next morning when Geraldine wakes Christabel as the bell is tolling, certain of the spell she has worked on her. Christabel greets Geraldine with perplexity over what has happened to her, feeling a sense of unknown sin, and after praying for forgiveness of that which she cannot understand, she then conducts Geraldine to meet her father, Sir Leoline.

They go to the Baron's room, and he greets this bright dame Geraldine with the kind of courtesy and welcome that would seem appropriate for a person of her dignity and grace. Sir Leoline grows pale when he discovers that the lady who has been his daughter's guest for the night is actually the child of his old and beloved friend Lord Roland de Vaux of Tryermaine. They had been dear friends in youth but had become estranged from each other. Sir Leoline decides that he will make atonement for the cleavage in their friendship by declaring Geraldine's abductors to be "base as spotted infamy," and by inviting them to his tourney court for combat. Sir Leoline takes Geraldine in his arms, and Christabel shudders. But she cannot, being spellbound by Geraldine's evil touch, explain to her father what ails her.

Sir Leoline orders Bracy the bard to go to Roland de Vaux of Tryermaine, and with music loud proclaim the safety of his daughter Geraldine, then to invite Roland to come and meet Sir Leoline and receive from him repentance for their quarrel and broken friendship.

Bard Bracy tells his lord, Sir Leoline, of a dream of evil he has had the night before in which he saw a dove-symbol for

Christabel - fluttering in the grass, "uttering fearful moan," bound in the coil of a bright green snake, and he asks the boon of Sir Leoline that he be permitted to delay his journey to Tryermaine for that day that he might go into the forest and purify it of any evil that might be there.

Sir Leoline hears Bracy only "half-listening," is generally unimpressed with the urgency of the plea, takes over the "plot" of Bracy's dream to the extent that he uses it as a **metaphor** for Geraldine's situation, interprets the dove in Bracy's dream to be Geraldine, not Christabel, and the snake to be the evil kidnapping scheme of the five warriors that imprisoned her - Sir Leoline had spoken of the five warriors as having "reptile souls." Geraldine's eyes shrink to a serpent's eyes as she looks at Christabel; Christabel is "in dizzy trance" from Geraldine's "look of dull and treacherous hate," and she begs Sir Leoline to send Geraldine away. Sir Leoline is humiliated and enraged by Christabel's discourtesy and inhospitality, feeling his name, his reputation, his fatherhood, his home dishonored by her behavior. He turns with passion to Bard Bracy, reprimands him for his delay, and sternly orders him to be about the business of his journey to Tryermaine. The poem ends with Sir Leoline and Geraldine leaving the room together.

"The Conclusion to Part II," for all of its importance as a gloss on the action of the poem, adds nothing to the story.

Question: What is the relationship between "The Conclusion to Part II" and the remainder of the poem?

Answer: Some readers say there is none. But, perhaps Sir Leoline looks upon Christabel with feelings of jealousy also, though perhaps not entirely for the same reasons. One might state the matter in this way: Christabel killed her mother in order that she, Christabel, might have life. In the first place such a hideous thing as this could happen only "in a world of sin," in a world where women have been promised pain in childbirth. We know it should not happen at all, and we can only explain it by saying that something is essentially rotten in the state of humanity. How could any father look upon so fair a creature as Christabel, knowing that she has been born only because his wife died, without feeling at one and the same time deep love and deep hate? Such a lovely creature should not have been born in such an ugly way! Such a lovely daughter would almost naturally become a substitute for the deceased wife, but then there is the further vexation of a recoil of guilt over incestuous feelings. And perhaps Sir Leoline is expecting Christabel to behave more like wife than like daughter in her disposition toward Geraldine. Add to all of this the fact that Christabel seems to be jealous of his embrace of Geraldine - and after all how often does Sir Leoline have the opportunity to embrace a lovely lady - and there is enough to cause Sir Leoline to feel rage, but then pity for Christabel because of his rage.

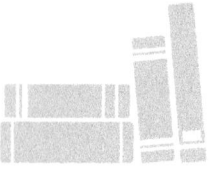

KUBLA KHAN

INTRODUCTION

....

This is probably the only poem of 54 lines in the literature of any culture that has had, in addition to numerous articles, four major critical books written about it: John Livingston Lowes, *The Road to Xanadu*; Elisabeth Schneider, *Coleridge, Opium and "Kubla Khan"*; J. B. Beer, *Coleridge the Visionary*; and Marshall Suther, *Visions of Xanadu*. Everything is known about the poem now except when it was written and what it is really all about.

THEMES IN "KUBLA KHAN"

Most critics assume that the poem is in part at least about poetry or about poetic experience, poetry as that which can be made (poesis), written down into readable form from the raw materials of inspiration, poetic experience as that which can be experienced actively by one who can relate himself to reality in a poetic way. The second of these subjects is inevitably an ambiguous matter for the critic, for the very good reason that the poets he writes about were themselves ambiguous. Another important possibility of subject matter and **theme** is that advanced by Carl R. Woodring. Professor Woodring emphasizes the importance of our deciding as readers whether the poem is in favor of Kubla or against him. If Kubla is considered to be a representative of the tyrannical struggle for power and wealth and luxury, the poet with the "flashing eyes" and "floating hair" in the last of the poem must be interpreted as creating somehow in contrast to Kubla, not in comparison to him. It is possible that the pleasure-dome with the caves of ice may have relatedness to excesses in Russian politics. Empress Anna of Russia not long before her death in 1740 had in a moment of whimsical luxury-loving decreed that a pleasure-dome be built of ice. The Empress subsequently ordered that a courtier who had earned the Court's disfavor marry an ugly woman and then that the bride and groom display themselves naked on a bed of ice in the mock palace that was the pleasure-dome. Such an incident would have had for Coleridge a very special repugnance during those years when he was directing so much firepower against ambition and tyranny. There were other such stories of iced luxury in the Russian Court. In the fun and games that Empress Elizabeth (and later Catherine) planned for her guests, there were rides in toboggans over mounds of snow that had been artificially constructed especially for thrill. At the end of each sequence of this aristocratic sport, the company was drawn to a pleasure-hut located on the highest of the mounds. William Cowper in Book V of The Task had condemned these consciously constructed luxuries. Coleridge would of course have known the literature in which the accounts of the Russian goings-on were given.

There may have been also in Coleridge's mind when he had Kubla decreeing the pleasure-dome the palace of the deceitful language of William Pitt. In describing the way Pitt's palace had been destroyed in Parliament by Fox, Coleridge wrote: "Like some good genius, he approached in indignation to the spell-built palace of the state-magician, and at the first touch of his wand, it sunk into a ruinous and sordid hovel, tumbling in upon the head of the wizard that had reared it.

Within this context of possibilities, the ancestral voices that prophesy war in the poem could be good, not bad, for this kind of luxury-loving, or this kind of deceit, should be expunged from human institutions.

IS "KUBLA KHAN" A FRAGMENT?

A good deal of the writing and speaking about "Kubla Khan" has centered on whether the poem is really a fragment or not. Coleridge started the discussion by calling the poem a fragment when he first published it in 1816. He did not stop with the sub-title "Or, A Vision in a Dream. A Fragment." He published a preface to the poem explaining that it had its origins in a dream and that the reason for its not being more of a poem was that after waking, most of the dream had faded from his mind.

There is good cause to think that Coleridge was lying when he explained the poem in this way. One reason for not believing him is that there are so many "apologetic prefaces" to his poems; the preface to "Kubla Khan" is not in purpose unique. He does much the same kind of apologizing for "Reflections on Having Left a Place of Retirement" and for "Fire, Famine, and Slaughter." Humphry House has commented on how much of Coleridge's work is marred by self - pity. Max F. Schulz has observed that Coleridge's prefaces tend to bias the reader's mind toward a work before he ever has a chance to read it.

If the preface to "Kubla Khan" is factual, it certainly has a large portion of the mysterious in it for a factual report. There is a dream of a visionary sort, there is a visitor who comes in very nearly the style of a vision, and there is the poem that comes out of a dream rather than out of any kind of conscious effort at writing. One becomes more suspicious of the validity of the "explanation" of "Kubla Khan" the further one reads into the Coleridgean canon. He is continually easing his own sense of failure about a work by giving some account of misfortune during the time that he was working on it.

Among the more well-known critics, J. L. Lowes, Meyer Abrams, and Elisabeth Schneider have considered Coleridge truthful in what he said about the origin and disruption of the poem. Those who consider him prevaricating in the account are G. Wilson Knight, Humphry House, and George Watson. Marshall Suther and Carl Woodring have taken a stand between the two poles in holding that whether an author considers a poem a fragment or not, it still can be a whole with regard to what it says.

THE DATE OF "KUBLA KHAN"

Elisabeth Schneider's book *Coleridge, Opium*, and *"Kubla Khan"* is the best source of information and suggestion for considering the date of the poem. She has eighty-four interesting pages on the subject. She begins by stating the two facts about the matter: we do not know positively when the poem was written; the poem had come into being by October of 1800. Miss Schneider argues for a later date than the one normally accepted; she thinks the best estimate is May or June, 1800. Carl Woodring supports the theory that it was written sometime during Coleridge's annus mirabilis, 1797 - 98.

THE STRUCTURE OF THE POEM

"Kubla Khan" has more regularity in versification, more consistency in meter than one might expect from the poet who wrote "Christabel." There are only a few places in "Kubla Khan" where Coleridge has used his favorite device, the anapest. Coleridge obviously exercised restraint in the writing of the poem, for the pattern that we have in the poem is certainly a tight one. The poem may easily be divided into seven sections:

lines 1 - 5: the location of the pleasure-dome

lines 6 - 11: a description of the whole area of the park

lines 12 - 24: the origins of the sacred river

lines 25 - 30: the geographical course of the river over the five-mile distance to the lifeless ocean

lines 31 - 36: further description of Kubla's dome

lines 37 - 41: introduction of the damsel with the dulcimer (stringed musical instrument)

lines 42 - 54: climactic lines of the poem that tell of the poet who will build with imaginative power the dome in air

If we call these divisions of the poem sections, we may call two larger divisions Parts: Part I is made up of sections one through five (lines 1 - 36), and this part relates to Kubla; Part II is made up of sections six and seven (lines 37 - 54), and they are about the poet with the "flashing eyes" and the "floating hair," his inspiration from the music of the Abyssinian maid, and his poetic architecture. The introductory sections in each of the Parts (sections one and six) have an equal number of lines and a similar pattern in **rhyme**. The two sections in the poem that are on the subject of creation or forces of creation, sections 3 and 7, are the longest sections and are equal in length, both having a dozen lines. The middle section in the poem, the one that connects up the river and the dome, is similar in rhyme scheme to section 2 (lines 6 - 11) and to section 5 (lines 31 - 36). One can also see at work much more than a vision-haunted poet, harassed by a Porlock resident, in such a technique as having the last lines of each of the two main sections of the poem so much alike in rhythm: line 36: "A sunny pleasure - dome with caves of ice"; line 54: "And drunk the milk of paradise." One may also observe that Coleridge makes conscious use of a different kind of meter when he does something so different in the poem as describing a natural scene and talking about the dome-building poet. When he describes the chasm, cedarn cover, fountain, and sacred river in section 3, he makes assiduous use of the loco-descriptive **pentameter** couplets; but then when he comes to the mystery of the poet who has fed on honey-dew and drunk the milk of paradise, he uses a favorite kind of meter for achieving chant - like effects, namely truncated **tetrameters** (used also in "Songs of the Pixies," "Ode on the Departing Year," "Christabel," and "Lewti").

The Crewe MS when compared with the finished product that was published in 1816 furnishes further evidence of Coleridge's labored artistry. Lines 6 and 7 of the poem in the Crewe MS read as follows: "So twice six miles of fertile ground / With walls and towers were compass'd round." The published form of the poem has: "So twice five miles of fertile ground /

With walls and towers were girdled round." The published version shows some pretty sophisticated opium dreaming. The sibilant s -sounds have been in three places edited out, and in the line "So twice five miles of fertile ground," the use of the i - diphthong comes in four different words. There is further a correspondence in accented vowels in "girdled" and "fertile" so that here is virtually a double **rhyme** in "fertile ground" and "girdled round." One other change from the Crewe MS to the published edition of the poem is worth noting in this discussion. Mount Abora in line 41 was in the Crewe MS Amara as in Milton's *Paradise Lost*. Coleridge changed this to Abora probably so as to avoid too great a contrast between dulcimer (sweetness) and amara (bitterness). To leave Amara at Amora, rather than moving the change further to Abora, would probably (amor) have created an unwanted allegorical association.

THE LANDSCAPE OF THE POEM

Coleridge in his preface said the inspiration for the vision that became "Kubla Khan" came to him while he was reading Purchas his Pilgrimage (London: 1626). The passage that Coleridge quoted is this one:

> In Xamdu did Cublai Can build a stately Palace, encompassing sixteen miles of plaine ground with a wall, wherein are fertile Meddowes, pleasant Springs, delightful Streames, and all sorts of beasts of chase and game, and in the middest thereof a sumptuous house of pleasure.

"IN XANADU"

The story has it that the Cublai Can of Purchas built a house of pleasure at Xamdu, Xaindu, or Xandu; John Livingston Lowes says Coleridge changed the name to Xanadu for the purposes of euphony. G. Wilson Knight suggests that Coleridge chose Xanadu because X would be symbolic of last things as A of Abyssinia - Abora would be of first things and as K would be of middle things. John Beer relates Xanadu to the fallen world and the loss of paradise. Humphry House holds the opposite view, saying that it is the most natural thing, given our normal human responses, unadulterated by the overly-sophisticated demands of high-level criticism, to take Xanadu as paradise. Marshall Suther in substantial agreement with House says that we are led to feel Xanadu is paradise by the tone of the poem; if Coleridge meant it to be a bad thing, he failed as a rhetorician. It is probably obvious enough that Xanadu would satisfy the need in a romantic setting for the far-away.

"A STATELY PLEASURE-DOME"

Elisabeth Schneider says that dome is a "self-echo"; Coleridge chose the word for its fullness of sound. Maud Bodkin associates the dome with Elysian Fields, J. B. Beer (the world of the poem is after the Fall) with Pandemonium, Woodring (see above) with the Russian ice-palace where perversely sensual pleasures were indulged.

Marshall Suther relates the dome in "Kubla Khan" with similar structures in many of Coleridge's poems. He considers the dome a kind of privileged retreat for experiences of inspiration, vision, delight. Most significantly the dome is at one and the same time continuous with nature but above it and beyond it. Douglas Angus in a study of love and guilt in Coleridge's poems comments on the dome as a breast symbol, the symbolic process being in line with Coleridge's narcissistic personality. The dome then becomes a symbol of security. Some critics have commented on the fire-ice juxtaposition in Coleridge's work generally as a means of approaching the dome as a structure in which are reconciled the opposing forces in the life of man - birth and death, creation and destruction.

"ALPH, THE SACRED RIVER"

G. W. Knight interprets the poem as an allegory of human existence, and the river consequently as the River of Life.

George Watson, rejecting Knight's interpretation, says "Kubla Khan" is a poem about poetry, and Alph is the river of the poetry of imagination. The topographical behavior of the River is like that of the imagination as Coleridge conceives it, taking inchoate matter and shaping it into a harmonious, meaningful whole. Humphry House has discussed the river in the terms of a life-giving source of fertility. The sacred river is an example of the givenness of life, of the abundance of life (as such it is sacred); but just because it is this it is dreaded, for it recalls all the unfathomable mystery of human existence. Still, says House, the river affirms the fertile garden of the world as the revered ground for human striving. Marshall Suther says the river is both the River of Life and the river of poetry. J. L. Lowes connects the River Alph with Alpheus and with the sacred river Nile. He refers to the account by Seneca of the vast sea that is hidden in the depths of the earth, the source of such rivers as Alphaeus and the Nile. J. B. Beer rejects the notion that the Alph is the river of Milton's paradise. He says that Alph, rather, is the sacred river after the Fall. He supports his interpretation of the river by noting that it can no longer return to the fountain, but, rather, in this world after the fall, it must follow a course down to the sterile sunless sea. Because the river is separated from the fountain, the fountain becomes destructive. Beer suggests also the possibility that the Alph is related to Alpheus, the male principle, who is forever seeking the female principle, Arethusa.

There are no definite relationships established in the poem between the river, the fountain, and the lifeless ocean, so says Richard Gerber. But considering that the sea is underground, and that it is called both sea and ocean, Gerber says it is possible to assume that it has a much farther reach than the five-mile course of the river. The ocean is underneath the fountain, the fountain may throw up the ocean, the ocean may be frozen (sunless), and the hail in the fountain's spout may be ice-fragments, all this amounting to a way out of sterility - a cyclical movement of nearly cosmic proportion that corresponds as a cycle of life and death to the cyclical myth of Attis and Cybele. Gerber suggests an association between the Alph (alpha - first letter of the Greek alphabet) and Cybele, the mother - goddess who represented the earth. He considers the association obvious enough in view of the traditional identification of the mother-goddess with the forces of fertility in the earth, here in "Kubla Khan," Mr. Gerber says, the fountain and the river. Water, he reminds us, has a universal identification with fertility. He recalls the tendency toward the equivalence of Cybele with Rhea, the Greek mother-goddess, and the fact that cross references in classical dictionaries send readers to Rhea when they are studying Cybele. Popular etymology established a correspondence between the Greek verb to flow and the name Rhea.

"CAVERNS MEASURELESS TO MAN"

Wylie Sypher suggests that Coleridge's caverns in "Kubla Khan" may recall his acquaintance with Cheddar Gorge near Nether Stowey and with the caverns at Wookey Hole. Dorothy Wordsworth indicates in her Journal that Coleridge made a visit with her and her brother to Cheddar on 16 & 17 May 1798. Tradition has it that the gorge near Nether Stowey was cut out by the devil.

Marshall Suther points out the "inverse correspondence" of the caverns with the fountain, the tumult of the caverns matching the turmoil of the fountain. Richard Gerber, pursuing the critical inquiry of possible relations between Kubla and Cybele, suggests an association of Cybele with the caverns. If the dome is considered symbolic of the male power of erection, the lifeless caverns may be considered symbolic of castration. Cybele was destroyer of fertility as well as the origin of it; she was known as a jealous goddess for whose gratification Attis and her priests castrated themselves. But beyond this possibility, Gerber says, is the greater one of Cybele as the immense womb, womb of earth, womb of birth, womb of death. Maud Bodkin indicates a relationship between the caverns in Coleridge's poem and the concept of the two worlds in Plato's *Phaedo*, the upper world and the under world. There is in Plato's picture a great cavern through the whole Earth, and all rivers flow into this cavern and out again

"A SUNLESS SEA"

Marshall Suther associates the sunless sea with death, with "eternal nothingness," and indicates the contrast between the sea and the vaulting fountain of life. He comments on the "near ubiquity" of the sea as symbol in Coleridge's poetry, and on the biographical element involved in the sea as symbol - Coleridge was an islander. The most powerful element in the sea image in "Kubla Khan" is its "boundlessness," compared with the established bounds in "Kubla's garden."

"FORESTS ANCIENT AS THE HILLS"

George Watson says Kubla's park is a combination of a wilderness and a garden, the natural and the artificial, the wild and the controlled. These "forests ancient as the hills, / Enfolding sunny spots of greenery," says Marshall Suther, show the combination in the poem of "the free and the formed," a combination present also in fertile ground and walls and towers, in sinuous rills and incense-bearing trees. The effect that the description has on the reader is considerably determined by this combination of ancient forests and sunny spots of greenery. There is here the effect of shelter and refuge. Douglas Angus has identified the words that describe the garden as "consistently feminine: 'fertile,' 'girdled,' 'sinuous,' and 'enfolding.'" With regard to sources for Coleridge's ancient forests and sunny spots, J. L. Lowes says Coleridge is remembering for one thing "inchanting little Isle of Palms" from William Bartram's Travels through North and South Carolina, Georgia, East and West Florida, etc. Elisabeth Schneider suggests that these forests came from Coleridge's sojourn in Germany. There are sunny spots of greenery in nearly all of Coleridge's poems. There are too many of them in his notebooks even to attempt to count.

"THAT DEEP ROMANTIC CHASM"

Lane Cooper and Howard Parsons have taken Coleridge to task for having the holy and enchanted both in the chasm, Cooper objecting to love of a demonic sort in a holy place, Parson saying that the words romantic, enchanted, haunted do not mix with holy. Marshall Suther objects to this sort of analysis, for it presupposes that the poem is either moral or logical - he says it is neither, although it could be both. Suther says the words slanted, athwart, cover give a sinister effect. The chasm is both "ominous and attractive." There is a "continuity between the garden and the chasm" that "is essential to the unity and the meaning of the poem." The chasm is ultimately ambiguous because it is a place in nature where one tries to come in contact with supernature. Trying to touch the supernatural in the natural is a risk of ultimate proportions. Carl Woodring considers the chasm the natural and the dome and the garden as the artificial. The natural and the supernatural are not to be considered as opposed since both are found in the chasm. R.H. Fogle considers the chasm a symbol of the supernatural, which is opposed to the "natural" garden. Maud Bodkin associates the chasm with Hades and therefore opposed to the paradise that the garden is. G. W. Knight finds in the chasm the romantic, the sacred, and the satanic.

J. B. Beer describes the scenery in this part of the poem as recalling lost paradise; it is able therefore to stir in the depths of man's self "at once the attractive and terrifying, the holy and haunted." The woman in the chasm who wails for her demon-lover is linked with the ambivalence of the natural scene and with the emotions of the reader. She is woman after the Fall of man; she is the human being afflicted with ambivalence. She fears the demon - lover she wails for, but, yet, she wails for him. The demon-lover is fallen man, a little lower than the angels but only a little above the beasts of the field. The moon over the chasm, Beer points out, is a waning moon: such a moon would not be present in a situation of the redemptive. Beer comments on the "wailing women" of the sun-worshipping religions: women wailed in Greece for Adonis, in Egypt they wailed for Osiris, in Phoenicia they wailed for Thammuz. Beer notes Coleridge's interest in "demon-lovers" in the literature of Biblical times. This part of "Kubla Khan" (the section about the chasm and the woman wailing) is antithetical to paradise, says Beer.

Richard Gerber criticizes Beer's interpretation, for it gives, he says, too much emphasis to fallen nature. Gerber calls attention to the fact that Cybele was goddess of wild, savage nature, of wild forests and hills. In route to identifying Cybele as "the best-known of the goddesses who wailed for a demon lover," Gerber calls to mind that the original shrine of Cybele was a cave located in the mountains of Asia Minor.

"A MIGHTY FOUNTAIN MOMENTLY WAS FORCED"

The fountain is the source of the sacred river, Marshall Suther reminds us, and because the river is sacred, the location of the fountain would be holy. Mr. Suther says that a place like the location of the fountain where one comes in contact with the origin of life (with which the fountain is associated) would not surprisingly be "savage, holy, and enchanted," for created life is after all an ambiguous blessing - none of us asks for it, none of us really knows how to cope with it when we get it, and none of us is ever absolutely willing to give it up, or prepared to. Finally, Suther calls attention to the fact that there are in Coleridge's poems a number of fountains that would readily be associated with inspiration, including Castalie and Hippocrene. George Watson also gives the reminder of how frequent the association is made in classical mythology between rivers and springs and inspiration. Humphry House speaks of the fountain as creating the "sense of inexhaustible energy," Douglas Angus as a familiar symbol of birth. Some critics have related the fountain directly to the paradise-garden in *Paradise Lost*.

J. B. Beer, however, does not consider the linking of the fountain in "Kubla Khan" with fountain in *Paradise Lost* to be appropriate. In Milton's poem there is nothing, he says, to identify a surging, pulsating fountain such as the fountain that one finds in the deep romantic chasm in "Kubla Khan." Besides, Beer notes, the geographical locations are obviously different: whereas the location of the fountain in *Paradise Lost* is in the paradise garden, in "Kubla Khan" it is probably, Beer says, away from the garden and the river-plain; Milton's fountain is on top of a hill, Coleridge's in the deep chasm. With references to New Testament literature as illustrations, the "well of water springing up into everlasting life" in the Gospel of John, and to "the fountain of the water of life" in the Revelation to John, and with the recollection of then earnest of the fountain to the Tree of Life and the disappearance of the fountain at the time of the Fall, Beer interprets Milton's fountain as a symbol of immortality. To the contrary, the fountain in "Kubla Khan" is intended as a symbol for that "which replaces eternal life," "a spirit of ruin." Beer comments that Coleridge's poems show an organized body of thought on the subject of fountains, and he suggests that Coleridge's interest originated in his study of Egyptian theology; Coleridge considered Egyptian religion to be cyclically oriented.

The importance of the presence of water in a natural setting that becomes an inspirational setting is evident in so many of Coleridge's poems. Coleridge draws on mythological lore in several poems as he makes reference to the springs (or fountains) traditionally associated with poetic inspiration. There is in water the function of sound: the sound of water is Coleridge's poems often acts as an instrument for aiding the poet's musing. In both the sound of water and in the sight of water, there can be the evidence of power; such power can serve as an analogue of creative power within the poet. Within the larger context of Coleridge's use of water in other poems, the fountain in "Kubla Khan" is probably more than anything else we might consider it, emblematic of poetic inspiration, especially so since it is associated in the poem with the woman wailing for her demon-lover (women throughout Coleridge's poems are involved in inspirational experiences) and with the intersection of the chasm with the cedarn cover (many, probably most, inspirational experiences in Coleridge's poems are midway on hills and mountains).

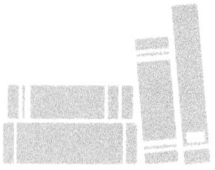

KUBLA KHAN

INTERPRETATION: THE MAIN THEME

"Kubla Khan" is a poem primarily about the inspiration of the poet, although, of course, it may be about other things also, as Professor Woodring's interpretations suggest. This poem brings together in one short work many of the familiar elements that are associated regularly in Coleridge's poems with the poetic experience. ("Kubla Khan" can for this reason reveal to us much about the process of poetic inspiration and creation as Coleridge thought of it with particular regard to himself as a poet.)

MUSIC AS INSPIRATIONAL POWER

If "Kubla Khan" is considered to be a poem primarily about poetic inspiration and creation, the emphasis should probably first of all be placed on the function of the Abyssinian maid and her music, remembering that in so many of Coleridge's poems music is associated with poetic inspiration and, as noted above, female figures of one kind or another are included in the inspirational experience.

The music the poet names in the poem, the music of an Abyssinian maid whom he once saw in a vision, is the imaginative force with which he wishes to build the dome. A number of statements by Coleridge outside his poetry show that he associated the functions of poetry and music. One of the most obvious statements comes in a notebook entry that Coleridge made probably sometime during the years 1807 and 1810. There Coleridge comments, "What is Music? - Poetry in its grand sense? Answer. Passion and order aton'd! Imperative Power in Obedience! What is the first and divinest Strain of Music? In the Intellect - 'Be able to will, that thy maxims (rules of conduct) should be the Law of all intelligent Being.'" (*Notebooks*, II, 3231, Text) The association here seems to mean that both poetry and music have the power of giving order to unordered materials through a creative act of energy or will. In making a marginal note on "the true poesy" in a copy of Tenneman's Geschichte der Philosophie, Coleridge expressed this ordering power in action as "the reducing of the rude materials of a multitude to measure and harmony." (*Notebooks*, I, 1057, Notes) In his essay "On Poesy or Art," Coleridge stated very nearly the same thing about music when he associated it with Art collectively. In his poems Coleridge so often cast poetic inspiration in the form of music, and so often used music in **imagery** to describe various aspects of the form, content, and effect of poetry. He would probably be able to think of the aeolian harp he owned at one time as having at least two important poetic functions: in the first place, the music made by the wind passing over its strings would be the flow of inspiration itself, as seems to be the case in the poem "The Aeolian Harp" - the wind become music evokes a vision; in the second place, Coleridge as poet could identify with the Harp, if psychological language is permitted, thinking of himself as a harp played by the wind of poetic inspiration. In "The Aeolian Harp" the poet seems to want to be both the wind of inspiration and the harp played by it. In "Kubla Khan" the poet wishes to be inspired by the music an Abyssinian maid plays, having seen the maid and heard the music in a vision he once had. It seems no mystery that Coleridge would have remarked at one point in the Biographia, "'The man that hath not music in his soul' can indeed never be a genuine poet." (*Biographia Literaria*, II, 14).

PASSION IN POETIC CREATION

The music that the poet heard in the vision of the Abyssinian maid, could he recover it (note the subjunctive), would stir him into a creating passion, a passion that would give him "flashing eyes" and "floating hair," a passion that would enable him to accomplish creation by fiat, that would so dumbfound and overawe "all who heard" that they would close their eyes "in holy dread" and "Weave a circle round him thrice. . . ." The inspiration for his power to build the dome would begin with the "deep delight" to which the recollection of the damsel's music would win him. The passage in "Kubla Khan" about the process of creation reads as follows:

A damsel with a dulcimer In a vision once I saw; It was an Abyssinian maid, And on her dulcimer she played, *Singing of Mount Abora*. Could I revive within me Her symphony and song, To such a deep delight 'twould win me, That with music loud and long, I would build that dome in air, That sunny dome! those caves of ice! And all who heard should see them there, And all should cry, Beware! Beware! His flashing eyes, his floating hair! Weave a circle round him thrice, And close your eyes with holy dread, For he on honey-dew hath fed, And drunk the milk of Paradise.

J. B. Beer thinks of the Abyssinian maid as a redemptive figure in the poem, as having the place of Queen Isis; she is therefore a complement to the woman in the cedarn cover who wails for her demon-lover beneath a waning moon. She is "a symbol of the lost tradition of knowledge for which mankind is seeking. . . ." The Abyssinian maid is in playing the dulcimer (a feminine instrument: Beer cites Burney's History of Music, which Coleridge had read) a complement to Coleridge also in his identification of himself with Apollo, who traditionally played the lyre (masculine instrument).

Richard Gerber points out that the priests of Cybele were famous for their wildly floating hair. He quotes a statement from Lucian about a false prophet by the name of Alexander: "He tossed his floating hair like a devotee of the Great Mother in the frenzy." Again from Lucian Gerber notes the phrase, "eyes flashing with great fervor and divine frenzy." There is nothing new, then, in the idea of the divinely inspired, divinely frenzied poet. If there is anything different in Coleridge's inspired poet in "Kubla Khan," it will be in the particular way Coleridge handles the matter of inspiration.

In "Kubla Khan" the "deep delight" is the basis for the creating passion. With regard to the process of inspiration, if such a mechanical-sounding term be permitted, what seems to happen in "Kubla Khan" is that the Abyssinian maid is herself a kind of poet, for she causes in him who hears her music, "The excitement of emotion for the purpose of immediate pleasure," if we may think of "immediate pleasure" as being the same as "deep delight," or of "deep delight" as being a heightened state of "immediate pleasure." The poet who creates the dome uses the inspiration of her music for producing something like "immediate pleasure," or "deep delight" in his hearers. The poet with the "flashing eyes" and "floating hair" is the center of the passion; those who would hear him have no such response as he would have to the music of the damsel with the dulcimer. He would create, but they would be able only to close their eyes "in holy dread" and try to exorcise the demon that possesses him. In the poem the Abyssinian maid plays music, but to her is attributed no such power as that of creating a pleasure-dome in air. Only the dome - building poet could become so possessed with passion that he uses it for an act of creation that is the apotheosis of "passionate order." He is the one in the poem who possesses a power of imagination that could be called, "Passion eagle-eyed."

THE POET AND THE I AM

It is evident in many places that Coleridge associates the power of the poet and the power of poetry with the creating Spirit and Power of God. One of the most pointed of Coleridge's concepts of the power of poetry (or the poetic experience) as having integral relationship with the power of God comes in a notebook entry from 13 October 1804: "To reconcile therefore is truly the work of the Inspired: This is the true Atonement - / i.e. to reconcile the struggles of the infinitely various Finite with the Permanent." (*Notebooks*, II, 2208, Text) The fact that the italics are Coleridge's would seem to suggest his awareness that he was using theological terms for poetic inspiration and creation. In the *Biographia Literaria*, Coleridge speaks of the primary Imagination as "the living Power and prime Agent of all human Perception," "as a repetition in the finite mind of the eternal act of creation in the infinite I Am." (*Biographia Literaria*, I, 202) These attitudes about poetic power being linked with or identified with the creating power of the I Am would certainly say something about the depth of despair that could come to a person who considered the power of poetic creation to be the power with which he gave life to the world in which he lived. Dejection about the loss of poetic power would really be dejection about the loss of the center of power, of life itself in all its relationships to Ultimate Reality, whether or not one uses for it the name God. Coleridge did at times speak of poetic power in obviously Biblical terms. In February, 1805, he wrote of "the Word - Logos" as "the profoundest and most comprehensive Energy of the human Mind." (*Notebooks*, II, 2455, Text) Logos is the name or title that the author of the Gospel of John in the New Testament uses for the pre-existent Christ. Only a few months later in 1805 Coleridge was making another note on the same subject, this time in very much the form of prayer: "We therefore record our deep Thankfulness to Him, from whose absolute Unity all Union derives its possibility, existence, and meaning...." (*Notebooks*, II, 2600, Text)

THE DOME, THE ABSOLUTE RECONCILIATION

The pleasure-dome is the central structure in "Kubla Khan" toward the creation of which the creator-poet with the "flashing eyes" and "floating hair" wishes to direct his power. If the reader could arrive at what the dome meant to Coleridge, he would of course have acquired an important help for discovering the meaning of this mysterious poem. The meaning of the dome in "Kubla Khan" might also furnish some important insight into the whole of Coleridge's conception of the poetic experience and the power of the poetic imagination.

An increasingly important source of information for the study of Coleridge's work is his notebooks. A great deal of space in the Notebooks published to this time is taken up by Coleridge's records of natural scenes he viewed. Though one must admit that Coleridge tried at times to view a natural scene in more or less the established way, his records of natural scenes can give us important information about how he as a poet wanted to relate to the nature that surrounded him, how he wanted to see the world.

In the notebook records of natural scenes, we find detailed accounts of Coleridge trying to put his imagination to work, the imagination not as an instrument for creating poetry in any usual sense of composing verse, but rather as an instrument for enlivening and ordering the world that he found about him. A study of the notebook entries concerned with natural scenes may shed interpretive light on the creative process in "Kubla Khan," for these entries are often about the attempt on Coleridge's part to project an inspired imagination into nature, to shape and modify it into a more meaningful form than its natural form presents. The idea in the passage copied into a notebook from some unknown source was a paramount one with Coleridge: "He who is most inwardly alive to the beauties of Nature, feels her most secret stirrings, cannot bear her flaws, and does all in his power to rectify them: he is putting into practice the essential truth and the essential holiness of all religions." (*Notebooks*, II, 3160, Text) That Coleridge considered a profound kinship to exist between the poetic and the religious is scarcely open to question. The problem in the discussion is to know what one means by the poetic, whether writing verse or relating oneself to the world in a particular way; the problem in reading "Kubla Khan" is to know what the dome is, whether the perfect poem (verse composed by one called a poet), or the world with all its multitude of diverse elements reconciled into a harmonious whole. In a good deal of Coleridge's work, both the poetry and the prose, the actual writing of poetry seems to be a by-product of another, more universal, more encompassing kind of experience; it is this more universal, more encompassing kind of experience that the notebooks can illuminate: it is this kind of experience that "Kubla Khan" may be principally about - the dome may be the poetic experience brought to its fullest realization. In a number of his poems, we seem to get versions of this poetic experience after it has been filtered through the processes of Coleridge's memory and contemplation, after it has been "recollected in tranquillity."

The famous principle of the reconciliation of opposites that Coleridge made such extensive use of in his literary criticism he applied as well in his notebook records of natural scenes. He shows a consistent desire to see the many diverse parts of a scene in relationship to the whole of the scene. In projecting his coadunating imagination into nature, he follows his own basic principle of the reconciliation of the many into one, the establishing of unity in the presence of variety. Applying this principle to "Kubla Khan" may show that the dome is the perfect reconciliation. The principle of the reconciliation of the many into one is everywhere in Coleridge's work. From his own account of a youthful experience with his father, it seems that he considered his mind from quite an early time "habituated to the Vast." Coleridge spoke several times through his notes of "the instinct of all fine minds to totalize - to make a perfectly congruous whole of every character. . . ." (*Notebooks*, I, 1606, Text) His numerous drawings of sights and scenes offer some evidence of his passion to give to each part its integral importance and yet to give to each a place in the larger whole. There is far more than an artist's curiosity or artistry involved - the state of unity in multeity is the establishment of the transcendent in the temporal, finding the permanent in the order of the mutable:

. . . how quiet it is to the Eye, & to the Heart when it will entrance itself in the present vision, & know nothing, feel nothing, but the Abiding Things of Nature, great, calm, majestic, and one. (*Notebooks*, II, 2045, Text)

Yet, the Eye and the Heart cannot know this quietness except after shaping the manifold variety of matter into the perfect whole. The vision does not come in surmounting the world of sense, the world of matter, not in using nature's furnishings as instruments to something higher, and then after inhaling their intoxicating perfume, leaving them behind as empty, burned out censers. The vision is found in the midst of the surrounding world (Coleridge is probably too Protestant to be a mystic) - it is "the present vision" - when the poet's imagination has shot itself forth as the creating Logos and brought "the rude materials of a multitude to measure and harmony." The vision is then an active one, not a passive one, for the poet's imagination creates it by working on the materials into which it is projected. It is not the snuffing out of the powers of perception, and the freeing of the self from matter. It is the active reconciling use of matter by the imagination, the bringing together of passion and order in the "true atonement," the reconciliation of "the struggles of the infinitely various Finite with the Permanent." For one who places himself in an I/Thou relationship with God, as is the Protestant emphasis, there is always the temptation to forget one's creatureliness and try to be Creator. The intimacy that God permits his creatures in addressing themselves to Him directly, rather than through a hierarchy of intermediaries, means that the creature is always in a position of risk; God's great love for the creature gives him the awful freedom to be a rebel - but ultimately the love of the God to whom Biblical literature gives testimony seems to be greater for the rebel than for the one who has no concern at all. Coleridge's most characteristic confrontation with nature is in the terms of an I/Thou relationship; he does not try to blend into it and become one with it, as a drop of water falling back into the sea. It is the I/Thou confrontation that characterizes the poet in "Kubla Khan" with the "flashing eyes" and the "floating hair." I would be difficult to consider him as seeking a mystical union with the Absolute.

In one sense the whole of the paradise of "Kubla Khan" is a reconciliation of a natural scene into a manifold whole. But, we are more concerned in reading the poem with what the poet says he would do if he had all the power he desired, more than with what he has done in creating the poem that we read. The would do is more important for revealing Coleridge's concept of poetic power than the kind of literary production that "Kubla Khan" is as a poem.

The dome is the one single creation toward which the poet says his energy would be directed. He conceives of a sunny dome with caves of ice. The dome bears likeness to a number of special places described in Coleridge's poems, more often sheltered places than not, where the opportunity for creative acts of power by the imagination can occur. There would seem to be in caves of ice a great supply of materials for the imagination to shape into delightful formations, perhaps "obelisks . . . pillars . . . rude statues of strange animals, episcopal Thrones, conical church yard monuments, reflected Lights. . . ." The poetic imagination could find an almost endless variety of materials with which to give nature a greater animation, and, in turn, to give the poet a paradise in the midst of this world.

But, perhaps the true significance of the dome for the poet is to be discovered first of all in its architectural form, not in any function that we might imagine for it. A close reading of Coleridge's notebooks reveals that the description he gives of natural scenes employ a number of geometrical designs. Many of these are similar to each other in shape and form. Following is a list of a number of those diagrams that Coleridge employed to express the contours of what he perceived: oval, ellipse, ellipsoidal, arc, cone, amphitheatre, half moon, semi-circle, arch, crescent, inverted arch, inverted crescent, bow, horse shoe, semicircular bason, perfect moon rainbows, bason-like concavities. These figures are used again and again, nearly countless times in the notebooks. Of the figures named above, the shape that is most obviously the shape of a dome is the arch. The figures given in the list are so prevalent in the notebooks as to suggest that Coleridge's most characteristic way of expressing the wholeness or unity of a natural scene with the variety of all its related parts was in some design of one-hundred-eighty degrees.

If we know that Coleridge in his efforts to describe the natural scenes he viewed sought passionately to find unity in the variety, to reconcile the many parts of the view into a oneness and yet give integral place to the parts, and if we know that the most recurrent of the geometrical designs he employed to accomplish this was a one-hundred-eighty degree arc, under one name or another, it is no unlikely possibility that the dome is the perfect creation of the imagination, the perfect unity in the variety, the most absolute reconciliation of the many different aspects of creation into the one perfectly related whole of creation. Coleridge characteristically did not associate the expression of energy with straight lines, as the foregoing enumeration of designs demonstrates. One of the entries in which the sky is described as a "soft blue mighty Arch, and called "an awful adorable omenity in unity . . . perfect union of the sublime with the beautiful," especially when compared to the shapes that Coleridge used to interpret his imagination's coadunation of natural scenes, would seem to support his association of the curve with energy. On one occasion he commented on "buildings, Wall, Garden" being "so slovenly in its

[sic] tyrannically strait parallelogram inclosures." (*Notebooks*, I, 1211, Text.) Perhaps on the same day that he wrote the entry about the sky, he expressed: my "Soul lies & is quiet, upon the broad level vale - would it act? It darts up into the mountain Tops like a Kite, & like a chamois goat runs along the Ridges - . . . ." (*Notebooks*, II, 2347, Text) Again, likely on the same day he wrote about the candle flame before him, "Its exceeding oneness + its very subsistence in motion is the very soul of the loveliest curve/it does not need its body, as it were." (*Notebooks*, II, 2348, Text.) It is certainly evident why Coleridge would say that poets were "the true Protoplasts, Gods of Love who tame the Chaos."

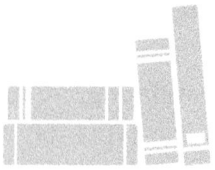

KUBLA KHAN

ESSAY QUESTIONS AND ANSWERS

Question: What is the principal **theme** of "Kubla Khan"?

Answer: Remembering (1) that the work of the poet, as Coleridge thought of him, is to bring form and meaning to the "raw materials" of nature, that poetry and music are associated in this creative act, remembering that this act of creative imagination requires the use of a passion that "unifies . . . by natural Fusion" to reduce "the rude materials of a multitude to measure and harmony," remembering (2) that this coadunating energy for Coleridge most often expresses itself in curved lines rather than in straight lines, we may interpret "Kubla Khan" to be about Coleridge as he would have wished to be, a vessel of power not unlike the Khan, creating by fiat, and becoming in the "Let there be" closely identified with the Divine I Am.

If the vision that Coleridge had of the Abyssinian maid playing her dulcimer would provide the music that would inspire the building of the dome, one poetic experience would become the basis for another poetic experience, the greatest poetic experience of all, really a poetic experience for every man, the world made perfect, in the astounding might of which every man would be transfixed in awe. The poet would be like the I Am or would be the I Am, establishing with his coadunating imagination the perfect unity in the midst of the perfect variety.

Question: Of what is the dome a symbol?

Answer: The creation of the dome is the perfect expression of creative energy, the supreme creation of the coadunating, esemplastic (remembering Coleridge's own words for the poetic power) imagination, the passion of creative energy exercised over nature in the creation of perfect order, "Imperative Power in Obedience," "the reducing of the rude materials of a multitude [of natural forms] to measure and harmony," the humanizing of nature, the absolute reconciliation "of opposite or discordant qualities," the diffusing of "a tone and spirit of unity, that blends, and (as it were) fuses, each into each, by that synthetic and magical power . . . Imagination." Keeping in mind that Coleridge thought of the creative act not ex nihilo (out of nothing) but as using the unordered materials already present in the universe, the dome is the sensual world made into the supersensual world, "an aweful adorable omenity in unity," a "perfect union of the sublime with the beautiful."

The dome in this interpretation is not the perfect poem, but the perfect world; Coleridge is not as much the powerful poet in the usual definition of the term as he is a man who wishes to live his life with such poetic power as to be a creating god. If "Dejection: An Ode" is a poem primarily about the failure of Coleridge's poetic power, "Kubla Khan" is no less a poem of failure - he cannot recall the vision, cannot use it for further creation, he cannot construct the dome. It is therefore not a failure at writing poetry, but a failure at something of much greater proportion.

Question: What bearing does "Kubla Khan" have on the much discussed matter of Coleridge as a mystic and visionary?

Answer: It is generally agreed (see Evelyn Underhill, *Mysticism*) that the mystic is one who desires to have such a vision that he can surmount the world, leave it behind with its imperfection and become identified with God. To the contrary, as is so evident in "Kubla Khan" Coleridge wishes to have a visionary experience as a consequence of his own creative energy, as a result of sending forth his own imaginative power and reconciling the variety of discordant elements surrounding him into a harmonious whole. Coleridge's poems reveal him more often desiring the power of the wizard than the submission of the mystic. It is significant, of course, that Coleridge in "Kubla Khan' anticipates the responses of others to the poet's creation in the terms of the demonic rather than in the terms of the divine. The poet's beholders would think him demon-possessed! For anyone who was aware of the Biblical attitudes about humility on the part of the creature toward the Creator I Am, it would be impossible to avoid apprehension about the desire to possess such creative power as the poet with the "flashing eyes" and the "floating hair" in "Kubla Khan" would possess. As suggested earlier, it is the peculiarly Protestant peril. It may seem more appropriate to talk of it as the Faustian peril, but, then, the Faustian peril is to a considerable extent the Protestant peril.

For the person who lives in the midst of the social and political order of time present, for the person who takes the present time seriously and wishes to reorder institutions of human society in accord with a basic personal relationship with God, there is not only the risk of not going far enough, but there is the risk also of going too far. The absolute necessity of the risk is probably the one most consistent emphasis of the theology of the Protestant Reformation. Coleridge's theological directions are consistently, if not clearly, within the main stream of Protestant thought. The creature is at one and the same time responsible for a serious encounter with all the problems and pain of the present, but he is responsible also to remember that only God's will is the ultimate ordering principle. Coleridge's poems often express the two sides of the Protestant dilemma. In the poetry of England previous to his time, the dilemma was probably only more eloquently expressed by Edmund Spenser in *The Faerie Queene*. The mystic wants to achieve union with God, to merge into the Divine Being; Coleridge wanted to control nature, modify it and transform it, reconcile through the imagination's unique power all its parts into a whole, shape what was there in nature into an earthly paradise. Politically he wished to do much the same thing. He did not wish to contemplate nature as only an instrument, as only a medium for achieving a higher, more exalted state of being, above and beyond the world.

It is not surprising that the dome-building poet in "Kubla Khan" bears a close likeness to the whale-hunting Captain Ahab in *Moby Dick*. Both are involved in the theological peril of the Biblical encounter between God and man. Both are taking the risk of confronting the world and its disorder. Their end may be mortal death, may be judgment as demon-possessed, but the Protestant Doctrine of Man interprets mortal death in the larger context of God's ultimate will. Mortal condemnation has not infrequently pointed toward eternal salvation.

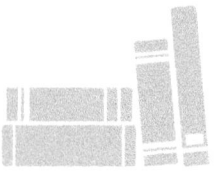

DEJECTION: AN ODE

INTRODUCTION

"Dejection: An Ode" is usually read as one of the most strategic documents in the life and work of S. T. Coleridge. The poem is often considered the last of Coleridge's good poetry, though he was to write a number of poems after 1802; it is generally agreed to be the last of his great poetry. Some critics interpret the poem as a most revealing account of the way in which Sara Hutchinson was integrally involved in Coleridge's demise as a poet. It will be observed that in the published version of the poem that one finds in collections of Coleridge's work, he addresses her as "Lady," "pure of heart," "virtuous Lady," "Dear Lady," devoutest friend. In one of the longest critical studies of the poem to date, Marshall Suther in his book *The Dark Night of Samuel Taylor Coleridge* says that Coleridge's failure as a poet is for essentially the same reason as his failure in love: he was seeking a religious experience in both, "a mystical experience of the absolute." The matter is probably more complicated than this. It will be useful in studying this poem to make a survey of the events of Coleridge's life leading up to and surrounding its composition.

COLERIDGE'S MEETING WITH SARAH HUTCHINSON

Sara(h) Hutchinson (Coleridge preferred the name without the "h"), sister of the woman who was to marry William Wordsworth, was the one great love of Coleridge's life. He met her at the Hutchinson home at Sockburn-on-Tees, located between Northallerton and Darlington, where Dorothy and William Wordsworth had gone upon their return from Germany. In October, 1799, hearing that Wordsworth was ill, Coleridge left Bristol and went to the Hutchinson home at Sockburn, accompanied by Joseph Cottle. Besides, Wordsworth was eager to see Coleridge for the reason that he and Dorothy had not yet decided where to make their new residence.

Students of Coleridge's poetry hear about Sara Hutchinson most often in their study of Coleridge's "Dejection: An Ode." The earliest draft that we have of the poem is in the form of a letter addressed to Sara Hutchinson on 4 April 1802. In a letter to Robert Southey 25 June 1801, Coleridge said of her, "the woman is so very good a woman, that I have seldom indeed seen the like of her."

A TOUR OF THE LAKE COUNTRY WITH WORDSWORTH

Coleridge's visit with the Hutchinsons was interrupted by plans that Wordsworth had made to tour the Lake Country. Wordsworth wanted Coleridge to see the places of his youth, and he wanted to locate a home for himself and his sister. Coleridge's records of the natural scenes they viewed on the trip are interesting for what they reveal of his quickened concern with his powers of description.

When Wordsworth and Coleridge left each other on 18 November at the end of the journey, Coleridge returned to the Hutchinson's home. An entry he made in a notebook on 24 November reveals that a love relationship between Sara Hutchinson and him had been established by that time. His poem entitled "Love" reveals his state of mind during these days at Sockburn. When Coleridge left the Hutchinsons, he went to London.

COLERIDGE IN LONDON AND SUCCESSFUL JOURNALISM

After much surveying of possibilities, Wordsworth and his sister decided to travel north to the Lake Country and settle there. Their new home was to be Dove Cottage at Grasmere, which Wordsworth had decided on in November. They moved there on 20 December. Wordsworth was never to be away from the Lake Country again for very long.

Back in London the Coleridge family were united again in quarters that Stuart, publisher of the *Morning Post*, had acquired for them. Between this time and June of 1800, when Coleridge would leave London and take his family with him to the Lake Country, he enjoyed reunion and reactivation of friendship with Charles Lamb; he established a relationship with William Godwin; he associated with a wide variety of people, publishers, writers, politicians, revolutionaries; he contributed poems to Southey's *Annual Anthology*; he wrote excellent, if not brilliant, prose for Stuart's *Morning Post*, denouncing Napoleon, opposing the Government and passionately opposing Pitt (see especially Coleridge's Character of Pitt); he wrote the "War Eclogue," "Fire, Famine, and Slaughter," a work directed against Pitt for permitting the inhuman destruction and waste of war by refusing Bonaparte's suggestion to negotiate for peace; he yearned for Wordsworth (as the Wordsworths yearned for him); he considered seriously where to move with his family.

This time of Coleridge's residence in London is remembered mainly because of his extremely successful journalism. His work for Stuart's *Morning Post* commanded respect from a great number, even those who disagreed with his ideas. E. K. Chambers in his biography of Coleridge uses a heading for his chapter on the years 1799 - 1800, "The Journalist." Coleridge discovered during these months the intellectual stance of a brilliant political analyst. (Students of Coleridge's work would want to study carefully his prose from this period.)

By March, 1800, Coleridge was missing the companionship of Wordsworth severely. "I would to God," he says in March, "I could get Wordsworth to retake Allfoxden. The society of so great a being is of priceless value." But the Wordsworths were settled, definitely settled; and if Coleridge wanted to be near them, he would have to travel north. Coleridge knew that Wordsworth would not consider a change. He felt the desire, the old but unflagging desire, to be engaged in some more imaginative, to his own way of thinking, more creative work. During all the heat of the political writing, with its brilliant flame and stinging sparks, Coleridge yearned for something nearer to poetry, if not writing poetry, then living in the visionary light of poetic experience. He was always suspicious of activity - a contorting tension in him - afraid that it would harden him, deaden him, that it would pull down the shades over those windows that looked out on chasms under waning moons and seas under sunless skies.

To talk about Coleridge as a visionary too often ignores his involvement in the dust and sweat of worldly affairs (the real weakness of such a book as Marshall Suther's *The Dark Night of Samuel Taylor Coleridge*). The other mistake is to overlook his imaginative immersion in visionary experience (a mistake one can greatly help himself to avoid by reading Suther's book). The only right critical approach to Coleridge is the one that encompasses him as poet, preacher, political philosopher, theologian, scholar, literary critic, an encompassing difficult to manage.

THE MOVE NORTH AND DECLINING HEALTH

In early June, Coleridge told Josiah Wedgwood that he was moving north. And toward the destination of Greta Hall, a house Coleridge had found about a dozen miles from Wordsworth at Grasmere, he and his wife and son set out on 12 June.

The real decline in Coleridge's health can be accurately dated from this time. The Lake Country and a drafty house were no place for a person with a rheumatic condition. But there was the compensating joy of personal friendship and renewed close companionship with the Wordsworths. There was again engaging talk about poetry. The year 1800 is the time of the writing of the famous Preface to the Second Edition of *Lyrical Ballads*, published in January, 1801. Coleridge struggled during the year to finish "Christabel," begun at Stowey in 1797, intended to be published in March, 1801, but not published until 1816.

The end of the year saw Coleridge in a bad way; his health had markedly declined. He was not helping himself any through exposure on long rambles to all kinds of weather. This is probably the time of the first real addiction to opium, of the first real enslavement to the drug. Coleridge made statements in 1814, 1820, and 1826 that he became addicted because of physical agony. He wrote to Cottle in 1814 of his addiction. But we know from earlier letters that Coleridge had used the drug before this year of real sickness in order to gain relief from emotional stress and to find what he had called once "divine repose." It is probably true, however, that the actual addiction of 1801 was closely connected with his breakdown in health.

THE DISINTEGRATION OF COLERIDGE'S MARRIAGE

There was the additional matter of the deterioration of Coleridge's marriage. It is, of course, only speculation to estimate what his unsatisfactory marriage had to do with his growing relationship with Sara Hutchinson. His marriage, in fact, had never been that good; it was, as we have observed previously, probably more Southey's idea than Coleridge's, although such a fact, if a fact, should not be used as justification. Mrs. Coleridge had never been a companion in mind to him. From various sources, Mrs. Coleridge's own remarks included, we know that she did not have that much respect for Coleridge, either as man or artist. She did not seem to have a capacity for comprehending his interests or directions. In much of the Coleridge - Wordsworth relations, she seems to have done little more than be tolerant; she never did really participate. She was bored by all the walking, by all the moving, certainly annoyed by Coleridge's too sporadic bread - winning. She probably tired of comparisons with Dorothy Wordsworth, though the comparisons may have only been made in her own mind. She was probably also aware that there was more than platonic friendship (though that may have been enough to vex her) in Coleridge's time with Sara Hutchinson at the Wordsworth's home in the winter of 1800 - 1801, the time when the love relationship between Coleridge and Sara Hutchinson found fullest expression.

When Coleridge visited for a month with the Hutchinsons in the summer of 1801, there was a turning point reached in his mind, which is not to say that he immediately made definite plans about a course of action. But after that stay with the Hutchinsons, his letters show more and more discontent with his present situation.

CORRESPONDENCE WITH SARA HUTCHINSON

The first of the correspondence between Coleridge and Sara Hutchinson was in January, 1802. In letters of 27 July 1802 and 10 August 1802 Coleridge makes professions of love to her. The one great poem to come out of this period of his life, and the poem that some readers consider to be the last of his great poetry, "Dejection: An Ode," was mailed as a verse letter to Sara Hutchinson on 4 April 1802.

These months, the middle months of 1802, were a time of continued painful agitation about his marriage. Strife in the Coleridge home continued, but any decision of a definite course of action was not forthcoming. The ups and downs of the marriage did not come to a real settling until four years later. At the time Coleridge came home to England from Malta in August, 1806, with his mind "halting between Despondency and Despair" because of his increased addiction to opium, he had decided in his mind that he could not any longer live with Mrs. Coleridge. In December of that year he went to visit the Wordsworths at Coleorton in Leicestershire, taking Hartley with him on the trip. Mrs. Coleridge was considering residence in the south. They were never to live together again. Coleridge's involvement with Sara Hutchinson was to continue for a number of years, though it was to remain for him little more than a futile passion.

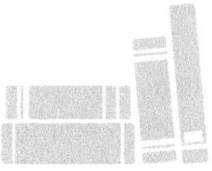

DEJECTION: AN ODE

THE POEM

Coleridge wrote "Dejection: An Ode" on Sunday evening, 4 April 1802. He likely went early in the evening to his study in Greta Hall, before the twilight had disappeared from the western sky. On that day the sun set at 6:33 p.m.: moonset was at 9:35 p.m.

Coleridge had recently heard the opening **stanzas** of Wordsworth's "Intimations Ode," and there is very good reason for reading these two poems for what they reveal of two poets' treatments of a generally similar **theme** - but one should not take the generally similar too far in reading the specifically different in the two works.

As noted above in the biographical study, the early draft of the poem "Dejection" was written to Sara Hutchinson as a verse letter. Almost half the verse letter is concerned with Coleridge's love relationship with Sara Hutchinson and what he hopes for her. The reader should permit himself the opportunity to see Coleridge at work as a skilled craftsman in poetry by making a careful comparison of the verse letter with the finished poem. The verse letter is available in the following sources: Ernest de Selincourt, Wordsworthian and Other Studies, pp. 57 - 76;

Humphry House, Coleridge, pp. 157 - 65; George Whalley, Coleridge and Sara Hutchinson and the Asra Poems, pp. 155 - 64; E. L. Griggs, ed., Collected Letters of Samuel Taylor Coleridge, Letter 438 in Volume II.

Stanza I

The poet is listening to a "dull sobbing" wind and looking at "the New - moon winter-bright! / And overspread with phantom light / .... / ... rimmed and circled by a silver thread...." (lines 6 - 12) He is in a state of dull pain, depressed, and lacking in the imaginative power necessary to act upon the world around him and give it life and meaning. The poet's condition and his reflections on it in **Stanza** I introduce the principal **theme** of the poem, and a theme with which we have found Coleridge so much occupied in other places, the relationship between the poetic imagination and surrounding nature, between the "shaping spirit of Imagination" and the sounds that have often stirred the poet and sent his soul abroad (Notice that Coleridge capitalizes Imagination.)

As Coleridge listens to the dull wind raking across the AEolian lute, and as he sees the New-moon, he remembers the weather forecast given in the "**Ballad** of Sir Patrick Spence." He has affixed a **stanza** of the "Ballad" at the beginning of the poem as a kind of motto:

Late, late yestreen I saw the new Moon, With the old Moon in her arms; And I fear, I fear, my Master dear! We shall have a deadly storm.

The **stanza** from "Sir Patrick Spence" tells that a new moon with the old moon visible within the crescent augurs a deadly storm. He thinks that if the composer of the "**Ballad**" knew his meteorology, the tranquil night in which he finds himself will not pass without busier winds than he now observes at work. "I see the old Moon in her lap, foretelling / The coming-on of rain and squally blast." (lines 13 & 14) Here in the first **stanza** of the poem, the poet says he wishes the storm to come: "And oh! that even now the gust were swelling, / And the slant night-shower driving loud and fast!" (lines 15 & 16) If the wind can only blow sobbingly, moaningly, as is the case now, it would be better if it did not blow at all: ". . . the dull sobbing draft, that moans and rakes / Upon the strings of this AEolian lute, / Which better far were mute." (lines 6 - 8)

Comment

As a poem about Imagination, "Dejection" is the record of a poet grappling with a question that he never really was able to answer conclusively for himself, the question of what happens in man's relationship with Nature. The poems and the notebook entries about natural scenes show Coleridge to be very nearly ultimately concerned with the problem of how much Nature shapes or conditions the life of man (perhaps we should say poet) and how much the life of man, more exactly the mind or Imagination of man, shapes or conditions Nature. For the power of the Poet to animate and shape Nature, see the following poems by Coleridge: "Life," "Happiness," "Lines on a Friend," "France: An Ode," "Lines written in the Album at Elbingerode in the Hartz Forest," "Apologia pro Vita Sua," "A Day-Dream," "To William Wordsworth," "The Night Scene," "Fancy in Nubibus," and "The Deliquent Travellers." For the power of Nature to animate and shape the Poet or man in general, see: "Life," "Ode," "Monody on the Death of Chatterton," "The Destiny of Nations" (lines 179 - 183), "On Observing a Blossom on the First of February

1796," "To a Young Friend," "To a Friend," "This Lime-Tree Bower my Prison," "The Dungeon," "Frost at Midnight," "France: An Ode," "To a Young Lady on her Recovery from a Fever," "Fears in Solitude," "The Nightingale," "Lines Written in the Album at Elbingerode in the Hartz Forest," "Lines Composed in a Concert room," "Hymn to the Earth," "Ode to the Duchess of Devonshire," "Inscription for a Seat by the Road Side half-way up a Steep Hill facing South."

Notebook entries that bear directly on this subject are the following: 798, 1189, 1376, 1471, 1489, 1498, 1510, 1589, 1592, 1597, 1603, 1607, 1610, 1616, 1668, 1836. The foregoing entries are all in *Notebooks*, I, Text. The following are in *Notebooks*, II, Text: 1996, 2012, 2013, 2045, 2052, 2087, 2208, 2344, 2356, 2357, 2402, 2406, 2414, 2818. This is only a representative collection; there are many others.

Stanza II

The first four lines of this **stanza** give further description of the poet's depressed state. They tell of a kind of pain (the "dull pain" of the last **stanza**) that is hardly a pain. Here Coleridge calls his predicament grief:

A grief without a pang, void, dark, and drear, A stifled, drowsy, unimpassioned grief, Which finds no natural outlet, no relief, In word, or sigh, or tear - (lines 21 - 24)

The reader should note carefully the splendid sequence of words used for the grief, all intended to emphasize the dullness, the depression of what the poet feels, or more accurately does not feel: "void," "dark," "drear," "stifled," "drowsy," "unimpassioned." In line 25 he uses two other words to support the description:

"wan," and "heartless." Lines 23 and 24 confess that there is no means of expression that will relieve his affliction. He addresses Sara Hutchinson, "O Lady!" He tells her of his despair, that he has had his gaze all the evening fixed on the western sky, but that he has gazed without being able to send forth the energy of his eye. The projection of his Imagination has been impossible; his eye has been blank:

All this long eve, so balmy and serene, Have I been gazing on the western sky, And its peculiar tint of yellow green; And still I gaze - and with how blank an eye! (lines 27 - 30)

He looks at the clouds above him, "in flakes and bars," at the stars, at the crescent moon, but he can only see - he cannot feel: "I see them all so excellently fair, / I see, not feel, how beautiful they are!" (lines 37 & 38) (Observe how Wordsworth uses the same words in the "Intimations Ode.")

Comment

One may find in this second **stanza** the first suggestion of the **theme** that will become more prominent as the poem develops: the Imagination of man is the source of Nature's life or death. This **stanza** anticipates the bolder statement in **Stanza** IV: "O Lady! we receive but what we give, / And in our life alone does Nature live: / Ours is her wedding garment, ours her shroud!" (lines 47 - 49)

Here in **Stanza** II the western sky, the clouds, the stars, the Moon are no less beautiful than before, but the poet can only see them "so excellently fair"; he does not feel their beauty, which means that his Imagination does not react to them and act on them. In **Stanza** VII he will see the wind, part of an actual wild storm, blow violently, but again he will only see, not feel how stormy it is.

Stanza III

This **stanza** introduces the first real note of ambiguity in the poem - one might say contradiction - and ambiguity that continues to the end, more or less on the one subject of the Imagination, what it is, what inspires it, what it is capable of.

In the first **stanza** the poet had asked that the slant nightshower come and stir him: now he says that he need not hope to find in external forces the force that can only come from within him. Because his spirits fail him, he cannot hope to find relief in the forms of natural beauty he sees: "My genial spirits fail; / And what can these avail / To lift the smothering weight from off my breast?" (lines 39 - 41) These in line 40 refers, of course, to all the natural forms he had named in **Stanza** II. Though he would keep his gaze fixed on the western sky forever, he could not gain the passion and the life that must come from within:

It were a vain endeavor, Though I should gaze for ever On that green light that lingers in the west: I may not hope from outward forms to win The passion and the life, whose fountains are within. (lines 42 - 46)

The statement of these lines would mean that though the nightshower came and drove loud and fast, he would not find the inspiration he craves. Observe the words used here for the Imagination: "passion," and "life," and observe that he thinks of them as coming from inner fountains.

Stanza IV

This **stanza** continues the discussion of where lies the origin, the inspiration of imaginative power.

Coleridge begins the **stanza** with another address to Sara Hutchinson: he tells her that Nature (all natural forms) has life only because the Imagination is shot forth into it as the animating and modifying power: "O Lady! we receive but what we give, / And in our life alone does Nature live. . . ." (lines 47 & 48). In more pedestrian terms this is to say that one gets out of Nature pretty much what one puts into it. It might not be such an easy confession for Coleridge to make; he would probably rather say that natural forms can send the soul abroad, can startle a dull spirit, "and make it move and live!"

At line 49 Coleridge takes up the **metaphor** of marriage, which he will use again in the next **stanza**, to describe the life that the Imagination can give to Nature. He says here in line 49 that whether Nature wears the wedding garment of joyful appearance and life or the shroud of sorrowful appearance and death depends on what the Imagination does to it: "Ours is her wedding garment, ours her shroud!"

Lines 50 - 53 comment on the kind of world necessarily experienced by those caught in the deadening struggle for wealth, fame, and worldly power: ". . . that inanimate cold world allowed / To the poor loveless ever-anxious crowd. . . ." (lines 51 & 52) They can only experience a dead world, a world in which nothing divine exists, a world without the beauty and glory of contact with the transcendent, an "inanimate cold world."

If one wishes to know anything of higher worth than such a dead world, from the Imagination must be sent forth a transforming power:

And would we aught behold, of higher worth, Than that inanimate cold world allowed To the poor loveless ever-anxious crowd, Ah! from the soul itself must issue forth A light, a glory, a fair luminous cloud Enveloping the Earth - And from the soul itself must there be sent A sweet and potent voice, of its own birth, Of all sweet sounds the life and element! (lines 50 - 58)

The suggestion is that one absorbed in the ambition for riches and renown cannot possess this transforming power (the "ever-anxious crowd"). Observe again the words Coleridge uses for this power: "light," "glory," "fair luminous cloud," "sweet and potent voice," "Of all sweet sounds the life and element!"

Comment

The paramount importance of the force called Imagination in man's relationship with the world (it is never clear in the poem whether Coleridge is talking about man in general or about that particular body of human beings called poets) comes through in what is probably the most daring line in the **stanza**: "And in our life alone does Nature live...." (lines 48) If the world is to be alive to man, if man is to be alive to himself, the Imagination must be alive. It is very nearly the same thing as saying that if one is to reconcile the discordant elements of his world into harmony, there must be a dome-building power in the Imagination, "flashing eyes" and "floating hair."

Stanza V

The **stanza** begins with another address to Sara Hutchinson, "O pure of heart!" Coleridge has in the preceding **stanza**, Stanza IV, used **imagery** drawn from music (frequent usage in his poetry) for describing the Imagination, "A sweet and potent voice, of its own birth, / Of all sweet sounds the life and element!" (lines 57 & 58) He takes up the same **imagery** again in line 60, "Strong music." In line 56 he has said that this music must come from the soul; here in line 60 he repeats that the music must be in the soul, "What this strong music in the soul may be!" Observe that he also repeats the use of light **imagery** for the power of Imagination: "This light, this glory, this fair luminous mist. . . ." (line 62) Now he adds the descriptive phrase, "This beautiful and beauty-making power." (line 63)

There is in this **stanza** the emphasis also that was made in Stanza IV, that this magical power is not available to any less than the pure in heart. Using the name Joy also for the Imagination, or as the name for the necessary spiritual state in man for the Imagination to exist and to be sent forth into the world, Coleridge repeats, "Joy that ne'er was given, / Save to the pure, and in their purest hour. . . ." (lines 64 & 65) Further, the new Earth and new Heaven that the Imagination creates in the present world (in Biblical terms, it has eschatological force) is "Undreamt of by the sensual and the proud. . . ." (line 70)

From the Imagination "flows all that charms or ear or sight." One thinks here of the wish Coleridge makes in the last **stanza** of the poem, Stanza VIII, for his devoutest friend, Sara Hutchinson. He hopes for her that she will find all things alive in the world, "To her may all things live, from pole to pole. . . ." (line 136) But the next line adds that if she finds them alive it will be because the animating force has gone forth from her into them: "Their life the eddying of her living soul!" (line 136) The last two lines of this fifth **stanza** say finally about the Imagination that all music that exists is the echo of that strong music in the soul, all colors that exist are the "suffusion" of that inner light. The message of the **stanza** is that the Imagination alone can make the world alive to us.

Comment

Strong music occurs at a number of strategic and telling places in Coleridge's poems. One could almost say that when the music becomes loud, either the poetry gets good or the poet intends something very important. The most immediate parallel to come to mind is, of course, in "Kubla Khan": "That with music loud and long, / I would build that dome in air. . . ." (lines 45 & 46) Other familiar parallels occur in "Chritabel" when Sir Leoline tells Bracy the bard to go "with music sweet and loud" to Lord Roland, and again when Bard Bracy says he will clear the "wood from thing unblest" "with music loud." (lines 485 & 528, 529)

One could interpret that the ambivalence we have noted in "Dejection" in the matter of man's interaction with Nature creeps into the lines in **Stanza** V, "Joy, Lady! is the spirit and the power, / Which wedding Nature to us gives in dower / A new Earth and new Heaven . . . ." Two principal interpretations seem possible; each one of the two expresses one of the views about man and Nature discussed above. The main difference of interpretation comes in deciding whether the word wedding has the function of a noun or of a verb in the passage. If wedding is taken as a verb, then the meaning is that Joy is the spirit and power in man that brings Nature to life through the process of wedding Nature to man; within the **metaphor** of marriage Joy has the function of the officiating clergyman. Nature is the bride, and the dower is "A new Earth and new Heaven." In this reading, Joy would be a synonymous term for Imagination, and would function grammatically as the antecedent of the pronoun Which. If one takes wedding to have a noun function in the passage, Nature is the agency of original action, the prime mover, within the **metaphor** the officiating clergyman that marries within man spirit and power, the state of such a union being Joy. The chief problem with the latter reading is that one is left with "A new Earth and new Heaven" as a kind of dangling construction. Within the structure and statement of these lines in **Stanza** I,

And oh! that even now the gust were swelling, And the slant night-shower driving loud and fast! Those sounds which oft have raised me, whilst they 'awed And sent my soul abroad, Might now perhaps their wonted impulsive give, Might startle this dull pain, and make it move and live! (lines 15 - 20)

the use of wedding as a noun would seem right and consistent. The greater number of lines in the poem, however, favor the reading of wedding as a verb. **Stanzas** III, IV, V, and VI all contain statements about the power of man coming from within man and acting on, shaping, enlivening the world around him. The yearning of **Stanza** I receives its most conclusive answer in Stanza III:

It were a vain endeavor, Though I should gaze for ever On that green light that lingers in the west: I may not hope from outward forms to win The passion and the life, whose fountains are within. (lines 42 - 46)

Any seeing of Nature will do nothing for him if he has not the power and spirit to respond, if that "shaping spirit of Imagination" is absent: "O Lady! we receive but what we give,

/ And in our life alone does Nature live: / Ours is her wedding garment, ours her shroud!" (lines 47 - 49)

Stanza VI

Coleridge was to make a most important distinction between Fancy and Imagination in his now famous critical work, *Biographia Literaria*, first published in 1817. But apparently at the time of "Dejection: An Ode," he was still using Fancy and Imagination as synonymous terms; we find them both in **Stanza VI**. Observe lines 79 and 86.

The principal statement of this **stanza** is that there was a time in the poet's life when suffering was only the raw materials that Imagination used in constructing a paradise in this world. There was a time when his Imagination was so courageous that it not only enabled him to confront the world with its usual share of discordant elements, but was so courageous that it did the dangerous, invited possible disaster, risked hurt, "dallied with distress." This was during those years when the Imagination was powerful enough to bring meaning out of chaos, harmony out of disorder. Of this time he says, "For hope grew round me, like the twining vine, / And fruits, and foliage, not my own, seemed mine." (lines 80 & 81) One pay profitably compare the "twining vine" herewith the "viper thoughts" in the next **stanza** (line 94) that coil around the mind. The difference he intends in the two states of soul is clearly there in the difference between the verbs twine and coil. What was in the past "fruits, and foliage" has become with the loss of Imagination "Reality's dark dream!" The change in him, he says, is owing to afflictions: "But now afflictions bow me down to earth: / Nor care I that they rob me of my mirth. . . ." (lines 82 & 83) So he says, but his real concern is there when he considers what has happened to him in his most precious self: But oh! each visitation [of afflictions] / Suspends what nature gave me at my birth, / My shaping spirit of Imagination." (lines 84 - 86) The **Stanza** seems to confess that there is some misfortune in the world powerful enough, ruinous enough, to subdue even the Imagination, however dynamic a force it is.

Lines 87 - 93 tell how the poet has compensated for the loss of Imagination. He hides his feelings from himself in philosophical pursuits, in "abstruse research"; he philosophizes his misery, he theologizes his loss of meaning. These lines are saying that he has taken up philosophy now that he has lost the power of poetry, but this is curious, extremely curious, for he is writing poetry, namely "Dejection: An Ode," commonly considered to be one of Coleridge's best poems. It is the standing problem of trying to know what Coleridge's means by poetry, whether written material composed by one who calls himself (or who is called by others) a poet, or a way of seeing one's surroundings and relating to them, perhaps so that in the seeing and in the relating, one's surroundings become infused with a nearly divine, a nearly transcendent quality.

Comment

Coleridge says in the paragraph just preceding the definition of the poet in Chapter XIV of the *Biographia Literaria*, "What is poetry?" This is so nearly the same question with, what is a poet? that the answer to the one is involved in the solution of the other." The diffusing, blending, fusing that the poet effects would not seem to be about only the writing of verse.

Besides the title of "shaping spirit" for Imagination, given in Stanza VI, Coleridge uses a number of other names to identify this power of creation in man. Those names are, "passion," "life," "light," "glory," "fair luminous cloud," "A sweet and potent voice," "Of all sweet sounds the life and element," "strong music," "Fair luminous mist," "beautiful and beauty-making power," "Joy," and "sweet voice." It is the voice of which "All melodies" are the echo, the light of which "All colors are a suffusion." It is the power that makes all things live "from pole to pole." (lines 134 - 136).

Stanza VII

This **Stanza**, the penultimate one in the poem, is centered around the storm, an actual storm that has developed during the writing of the former six **stanzas** and a storm that the poet now actually hears. Now he turns from the "viper thoughts" that have occupied him in **Stanza** VI to listen to this wind.

Of course, any reading of this **Stanza** should give close attention to Coleridge's interpretation of the wind. It is not only the force that he hears about him, but it also becomes the organizing **metaphor** in the **Stanza**; in fact, it makes **Stanza** VII virtually a poem in its own right. This stanza should also be read painstakingly for the revelations it can give about Coleridge's ambivalence toward the inspirational force he desires. In this regard, it should be read with **Stanza** I in mind.

Remembering that in **Stanza** I the poet had asked for a storm wind, now in **Stanza** VII when he gets it (the storm, within the time sequence of the poem, has developed in the time intervening since **Stanza** I), he cannot endure what it brings to him. He had expressed himself as desiring a storm wind to come and stir him, move him out of the dull pain that oppresses him (see **Stanza** I, lines 15 & 16) But now that the storm is upon him, he can hear in it only sounds of human tragedy and misery.

Besides hearing the wind as it passes over the AEolian lute as "a scream / Of agony by torture lengthened out" (lines 97 - 99), he hears in the storm wind the agonized sounds of a retreating army:

What tell'st thou now about? 'Tis of the rushing of an host in rout, With groans, of trampled men, with smarting wounds - At once they groan with pain, and shudder with the cold!

And all that noise, as of a rushing crowd, With groans, and tremulous shudderings.... (lines 110 - 116)

Though in a less tempestuous gust, there is the equally agonized sound of a little girl lost from her mother (some say Coleridge is thinking of Wordsworth's Lucy):

of a little child Upon a lonesome wild, Not far from home, but she hath lost her way; And now moans low in bitter grief and fear, And now screams loud, and hopes to make her mother hear. (lines 121 - 125)

(Notice that the pathos of the incident of the lost child is heightened by Coleridge by his having her "Not far from home...." [line 123].)

Given the poet's kinds of responses now that the wished-for-wind has come, the **Stanza** seems to support the earlier confession by him that one "may not hope from outward forms to win / The passion and the life, whose fountains are within." (lines 45 & 46) The storm-wind cannot be anything meaningful unless the Imagination acts upon it.

But the whole matter is more ambiguous than this. If there is any one **stanza** in the whole of Coleridge's poetry that a reader should not oversimplify, it is this one, **Stanza** VII of "Dejection." Although the wind sounds to him like "a scream / Of agony by torture lengthened out," like the painful rushing of a routed army, like the screams of a lost child for its mother, still he pays the wind the highest tribute that he could give to any force, natural, human, or superhuman, "Thou mighty Poet, e'en to frenzy bold!" In fact, read in relationship with a number of Coleridge's other poems, it would seem even more accurate to say that Coleridge addresses the wind as "mighty Poet" not in spite of what he hears in it, but, rather, because of what he hears. The wind is frequently present in places of inspirational experiences in Coleridge's poetry and is inspiring because it is perilous. (Further discussion of this matter below in "Comment.")

The particular places with which Coleridge associates the wind should be noted: "Bare crag, or mountain-tairn, or blasted tree, / Or pine-grove whither woodman never clomb, / Or lonely house, long held the witches' home. . . ." (lines 100 - 102)

Comment

For the further illumination of the character of the wind as an inspirational force as Coleridge conceived it, and of the inspirational experience as it occurs in his poems, we may profitably compare the settings in "Dejection: An Ode" with those in other poems.

Coleridge wrote to Robert Southey at one o'clock on the morning of 3 November 1794 that Schiller's "The Robbers" had so disturbed him that he trembled like an aspen leaf. "To the Author of 'The Robbers'" (1794) is Coleridge's tribute to Schiller for this stirring work. The poem contains an inspirational setting that is very nearly a projection of the situation in which Coleridge read the work. Coleridge read "The Robbers" on a Winter midnight when the wind was high. Coleridge has Schiller's "loftier mood" of inspiration in the evening with a tempest blowing through the woods. Most experiences of poetic inspiration in Coleridge's poetry are evening experiences, and there are a great number of them set in woods, with strong winds rushing and moaning through the branches of the trees. The phrases that Coleridge makes use of in this poem to describe the inspirational encounters of Schiller with the afflatus and of himself with Schiller could be used as an index to a number of such experiences to which Coleridge's poems give testimony: "loftier mood," "finely-frenzied eye," "tempest-swinging wood," "mute awe gazing," "weep aloud," "wild ecstasy."

Alike the time and circumstance of his reading of Schiller, the higher inspirational setting to which Coleridge directs Joseph Cottle in "To the Author of Poems" (1795) is at midnight with a tempest. The passion of poetic feeling is intensified by the peril of the place. It is in the higher regions named in "To the Author of Poems" that "th'" impassioned **theme**" is sung. Bidding Cottle "Strong, rapid, fervent" to flash "Fancy's beam," Coleridge directs him to the higher place, "those richer views among." But the higher place is not a place of calm; it is in fact a place of more passion than Virtue and Truth require: "Virtue and Truth shall love your gentler song; / But Poesy demands th' impassion'd theme." (lines 39 & 40) The place of impassioned poetry is a place of awful sight and sound, the place of "cloud - climb'd rock, sublime and vast, / That like some giant kind, o'er-glooms the hill," the place where "the Pine-grove to the midnight blast / Makes solemn music!" (lines 19 - 22) But, though one cannot expect to find the quiet and peaceful there, one can expect to find sweetness. When the fading light of day gleams softly down the sky, the sweet scent of ripe fruit fills the evening air: "Waked by Heaven's silent dews at Eve's mild gleam / What balmy sweets Pomona breathes around!" (lines 41 & 42) The redolence of the fruit is not all; it is a place of harvest, and significantly is such just because it is not a place of calm: "But if the vext air rush a stormy storm / Or Autumn's shrill gust moan in plaintive sound, / With fruits and flowers she loads the tempest-honor'd ground." (lines 43 - 45) The reader should note carefully that the ground is tempest-honor'd. The soul of Coleridge's counsel to Cottle and the most important statement he makes in the poem about poetic inspiration is that the "vext air," "the shrill gust" reap the greatest harvest of fruit. The inspirational domain for the higher poetry is fraught with the wild, the precarious, the frightening; it is the wild wind that sends the poet's soul abroad - or that should do so.

Each of the three titles that Coleridge gives to the wind in "Dejection" suggests that it is a force that can move beyond the mortal limits of sanity and security: "Mad Lutanist," "Thou Actor, perfect in all tragic sounds," "Thou mighty Poet, e'en to frenzy bold." Here is the frenzied dome-building poet of "Kubla Khan" in another dress, not striking his listeners down with "flashing eyes" and "floating hair" - but this time making "Devils' yule, with worse than wintry song, / The blossoms, buds, and timorous leaves among." (lines 106 & 107) It is not only that he desires the wind to be an inspirational force to move him out of his lethargy, but that he identifies with the wind to such an extent that he would desire to be the wind, had he the strength to bear its revelations, the toughness to endure what it knows, the power to know what it knows and to modify the discordant elements of that greater knowledge into a larger harmonious whole. He would not, had he the stability that he wishes for Matilda Betham, be content only to receive the wind as inspirational force, as if he were the AEolian lute whose strings are set in motion by the wind passing over it. He would move even closer to the heart of things, closer to the core of meaning of life and death, closer to the crux of the universe. Had he the guts of Captain Ahab, he would seek out Moby Dick. He would move into the gale and gust of the whirlwind of inspiration if he had the courage to face what he hears. This is just the cul-de-sac in the inspirational experience to which Coleridge comes: the very force that could inspire him, lift him, stir him, threatens to tell him so much about the real blackness at the heart of things that he cannot endure the inspiration when it comes. He asks to face the terrible secrets of the universe, and then to live poetically in the midst of them, modifying them, transforming them, coadunating them. But the force of revelation threatens to show him to reality that he cannot bear, threatens to tell him a truth about existence that would make existence too meaningless to endure. This is the "Dejection" crisis, this is the loss of power that the poem laments. The "Dejection" crisis is not being unable to write poetry -he is doing that very well in "Dejection: An Ode" - it is being unable to take the black truth about one's terrifyingly dangerous place in a chaotic universe and make harmony out of it. This is obviously a crisis in a much larger, in a much greater concern than writing poetry.

Stanza VIII

The preceding seven **stanzas** have occupied the poet for half the night. It seems fitting that he should have come at the end of **Stanza** VII to the darkest hour and not to sleep: "'Tis midnight, but small thoughts have I of sleep...." (line 126) This concluding **stanza** of the poem is a prayer in Sara Hutchinson's behalf. He hopes for her peaceful sleep, health, inner calm, and joy:

Visit her, gentle Sleep! with wings of healing, And may this storm be but a mountain-birth,

With light heart may she rise, Gay fancy, cheerful eyes,

... friend devoutest of my choice, Thus mayest thou ever, evermore rejoice. (lines 128 & 129; 132 & 133; 138 & 139)

But the essence of Coleridge's prayer for Sara Hutchinson is that she may be able to overcome any such "Dejection" crisis as he has known, and therefore the most essential lines in **Stanza** VIII are these:

Joy lift her spirit, joy attune her voice; To her may all things live, from pole to pole, Their life the eddying of her living soul! (lines 134 - 136)

Lines 134 - 136 in this **Stanza**, Stanza VIII, contain the final statement of the poem on the subject of the power of the Imagination in relationship with Nature. All things will live for Sara Hutchinson because of her living soul. Note again lines 135 & 136: "To her may all things live, from pole to pole, / Their life the eddying of her living soul!" These two lines give the best gloss we could have on those difficult, complex lines in **Stanza** V:

Joy, Lady, is the spirit and the power, Which wedding Nature to us gives in dower A new Earth and new Heaven, Undreamt of by the sensual and the proud - (lines 67 - 70)

The Imagination weds Nature to us, the Imagination makes the marriage possible, and the dower we receive is a new Earth and new Heaven.

Finally, we may observe in **Stanza** VIII the emphasis on purity of heart as the condition or precondition of the Imagination, an emphasis that is recurrent in the poem. One of the principal reasons (if not the principal one) that Sara Hutchinson can experience Joy in the complex sense that Coleridge means the term is that she is "simple spirit, guided from above...." (line 137)

Comment

Humphry House has emphasized the relationship between the "joy" of "Dejection: An Ode" and the "deep delight" of "Kubla Khan." He cites two notebook entries that demonstrate the intimate links in Coleridge's mind between joy and the creative process:

Sunday, November 1, 1801. Hartley [Coleridge's young son] breeched - dancing to the jingling of the money - but eager & solemn Joy, not his usual whirl-about gladness - but solemn to & fro eager looks, as befitted the importance of the aera. (*Notebooks*, I, 1001, Text)

I write melancholy, always melancholy: you will suspect that it is the fault of my natural Temper. Alas! no. - This is the great Cross in that my Nature is made for Joy - impelling me to Joyance - and I never - never can yield to it. - I am a genuine Tantalus - (*Notebooks*, I, 1609, Text)

I. A. Richards has called attention to the excellence in **imagery** of the word eddying. He quotes a passage from the *Biographia Literaria* that serves as a gloss on the image, and that may serve also to expand our understanding of what it would mean for Coleridge to call Sara Hutchinson "O simple spirit."

They and they only can acquire the philosophic imagination, the sacred power of self-intuition, who within themselves can interpret and understand the symbol, that the wings of the air-sylph are forming within the skin of the caterpillar.... They know and feel, that the potential works in them, even as the actual works on them! In short, all the organs of sense are framed for a corresponding world of sense; and we have it. All the organs of spirit are framed for a correspondent world of spirit: though the latter organs are not developed in all alike. But they exist in all, and their first appearance discloses itself in the moral being.

(*Biographia Literaria*, I, p. 167)

Harold Bloom speaks of the figure of the eddy in the last **Stanza** as "inseparably both image and argument." He says it gathers up all the subordinate **imagery** in the poem. He calls attention to the linkage in Coleridge's thinking of the Imagination with the creating I Am. Coleridge makes his most pointed statement on the connection in the final chapter of Volume I of the Biographia:

The Imagination then, I consider either as primary, or secondary. The primary Imagination I hold to be the living Power and prime Agent of all human Perception, and as a repetition in the finite mind of the eternal act of creation in the infinite I AM. The secondary Imagination I consider as an echo of the former, co-existing with the conscious will, yet still as identical with the primary in the kind of its agency, and differing only in degree, and in the mode of its operation. It dissolves, diffuses, dissipates, in order to recreate; or where this process is rendered impossible, yet still at all events it struggles to idealize and to unify. It is essentially vital, even as all objects (as objects) are essentially fixed and dead.

(*Biographia Literaria*, I, p. 202)

"Dejection: An Ode" is the one work in the Coleridge canon that gives the most extensive poetic statement of the character of the Imagination.

DEJECTION: AN ODE

ESSAY QUESTIONS AND ANSWERS

Question: Discuss the principal **imagery** in "Dejection: An Ode."

Answer: For all that "Dejection" tells about Coleridge's life as man and poet, it is not a poem of entirely new subject matter or of entirely new **imagery**. It gives expression to **themes** and ideas that appear in one form or another (although, of course, not in as developed a form) in earlier poems and in later ones. The central **imagery** in "Dejection" is probably that of music.

Besides the title of "shaping spirit" for Imagination, given in **Stanza** VI of "Dejection," Coleridge uses a number of other names to identify this power of creation in man. Those names are: "passion," "life," "light," glory," "fair luminous cloud," "A sweet and potent voice," "Of all sweet sounds the life and element," "strong music," "fair luminous mist," "beautiful and beauty-making power," "Joy," and "sweet voice." It is the voice of which "All melodies" are the echo, the light of which "All colors are a suffusion." It is the power that makes all things live: ". . . Joy lift her spirit, joy attune her voice; / To her may all things live, from pole to pole, / Their life the eddying of her living soul!" (lines 134 - 136) Also in the passages in which Coleridge speaks directly about what the Imagination is and what it does, his **imagery** is constituted of music and light:

> Ah! from the soul itself must issue forth A light, a glory, a fair luminous cloud Enveloping the Earth - And from the soul itself must there be sent A sweet and potent voice, of its own birth, Of all sweet sounds the life and element! (lines 53 - 58)

> O pure of heart, thou need'st not ask of me What this strong music in the soul may be! What, and wherein it doth exist, This light, this glory, this fair luminous mist, This beautiful and beauty-making power. (lines 59 - 63)

> Joy is the sweet voice, Joy the luminous cloud - We in ourselves rejoice! And thence flows all that charms or ear or sight, All melodies the echoes of that voice, All colors a suffusion from that light. (lines 71 - 75)

The names for Imagination and the passages cited above might very well raise the question of why music any more than light is the central **imagery** in "Dejection." In the titles and lines here quoted from the poem, there is an almost equal use of music and light, coming to a kind of summary expression in the lines: "All melodies the echoes of that voice, / All clouds a suffusion from that light." (lines 74 & 75) But, considering the poem in its larger dimensions, it will be seen that Coleridge in **Stanzas** I and VII uses music, however harsh and foreboding, to describe the loss of, the absence of Imagination.

Light is conjoined with the predominant **imagery** of music in the poem. To recall, Imagination is described in telling phrases, the "fair luminous cloud," and what is the same, the "fair luminous mist." It is the power through which all things assume a shape and aspect of beauty that never before was theirs. The kind of light associated with the Poet's deprivation of this power is equally telling. Coleridge conjoins the "dull sobbing draft" on the Aeolian lute with the light of the moon, not a "fair luminous" light, but a phantom light:

> ... the dull sobbing draft, that moans and rakes Upon the strings of this AEolian lute, Which better far were mute. For lo! the New-moon winter bright! And overspread with phantom light, (With swimming phantom light o'erspread But rimmed and circled by a silver thread).... (lines 6 - 12)

It is the light of bad omen.

Question: What is the attitude expressed in "Dejection" about man's relationship with Nature?

Answer: As a poem about Imagination, "Dejection" is the record of a poet grappling with a question that he never really was able to answer conclusively for himself, the question of what happens in man's relationship with Nature. One should be careful not to oversimplify the Romantics' attitudes toward Nature. (For help in this strategic area of interpretation, see David Ferry's book on Wordsworth, titled *The Limits of Mortality*.) Coleridge started asking the question in his poetry before his twentieth year.

To be fair, there is an ambiguity in "Dejection: An Ode" about man's interaction with Nature. The weight of evidence in the poem is, however, in favor of the view that Imagination is more the shaping power over Nature than Nature is over the Imagination. This is probably the conclusion that one would reach about the comments that Coleridge made on the same subject in his notebooks. But even there he is cognizant of the great force that Nature exercises over him.

Finally, it seems that the matter of the reciprocal relationship between man and Nature as Coleridge's writings witness to it can be discussed only in the terms of relative degree. He never made a final statement either in his poetry or prose that was not in some way mitigated by another statement. Coleridge perhaps was not clear in his own mind how much influence Nature had on the mind or Imagination of man and how much influence the mind or Imagination of man had on Nature. But, the greater evidence reveals that Coleridge considered the Imagination to be the highest concentration of creative energy in the universe. It was Coleridge's confidence in a power in man that modified the external world that seems to have inspired his rejection of the empiricism of John Locke. Put theologically, God may act in Nature or be in Nature, but He acts most directly and most forcibly through the Imagination.

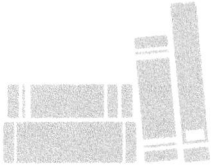

SAMUEL TAYLOR COLERIDGE

WHAT CRITICS HAVE SAID

THE SUCCESS OR FAILURE OF COLERIDGE

Coleridge's capacity for both delighting and annoying is probably unique in the history of English letters, unique because readers often feel at one and the same time delight at what he has done and annoyance with what he left undone. Generally, people, both companions and readers, have loved Coleridge, but there is the trend in criticism to discuss at considerable length "the failure of Coleridge." Praise of his poetry, particularly wiMh regard to "Kubla Khan" and "Christabel," usually includes some kind of reprimand for Coleridge's having left the works in the state that we as readers have received them. Coleridge was himself aware of his tendency to project large writing and publishing schemes and not to carry through with them, to leave the important hard work undone in the midst of a glorious daydream of what might be. He spoke at times candidly of this trait in himself.

It is true that the canon of Coleridge's poetry is modest in size when compared to that of other major poets, say Wordsworth, Shelley, Byron. But, this fact must be juxtaposed with the no-less-important fact of how many works of another kind he did. There are many critics who say that his contributions to the development of Christian theology in England and America far surpass in significance anything he did as a poet. There are some critics who acclaim his achievements in literary criticism more important than his achievements in poetry.

As suggested elsewhere in this study, what we seem to mean when we talk about Coleridge as a failure is that he did not write more poems like "The Ancient Mariner," that he did not do something more with "Kubla Khan," that he did not "finish" "Christabel." But this is dangerous language also, for in one very real sense these works are finished. We would have wished also that he had cleaned up the *Biographia Literaria*, given it more order and made it more readable. We would have been happier with the man if he had gone on and worked hard at bringing to realization some of the great, inclusive works he daydreamed about writing. When critics talk about the "failure" of the man, they obviously mean more than anything else the extent of his unrealized potential.

But there is no doubting the great influence Coleridge exercised over his contemporaries. One recent critic has said that Coleridge's impress on those who came to hear him lecture must have been something like what one would find in having Paul Tillich and T. S. Eliot combined into one person. One has only to look at the comments Coleridge's contemporaries made about him to know that he was not only an extraordinary man, but one who could leave a deep stamp on the moral and intellectual life of those around him. As an effort at illustrating his position in the estimate of his contemporaries and in that of some later important figures in the thought and life of England, there are given below extracts from statements made about Coleridge. They are arranged in a chronological order so that the reader may get a sweeping view of opinion over a period of about one-hundred years.

PRESENT STATE OF COLERIDGE STUDIES

There has been a kind of Coleridge revival in recent years. John Livingston Lowes increased the flow of traffic when in the late twenties of our century he cut the ribbon on the Road to Xanadu. The last fifteen years have found us reading in English alone nearly a dozen book-length studies of Coleridge as poet, literary critic, critic of society, and religious thinker. Leaving room, the usual and expected room, for necessary analyses of the poet's limitations, the books have been on the whole admiring of Coleridge's gifts, and achievements. In fact, when one permits the impressions of those books to have the maturing sun of a few month's active residence in one's mind, one feels in remembering them that the admiration of the critics for the poet has not seldom reached the proportions of awe.

HUMPHRY HOUSE

Everyone seems to agree that "The Clark Lectures" of Humphry House, published under the title Coleridge, are one of the best critical contributions of recent times. House has tried to see Coleridge as a whole man, which, considering the nature of the subject, is heroic indeed. House's analyses of the poems are considered admirable, as are his psychological insights into Coleridge's character.

THE SEARCH FOR SOURCES

Lowes' book on Coleridge's reading, *The Road to Xanadu*, has caused most of us to look upon the poet with about as much wonder as that with which we read his so-called "magical" poems. Several other books and a number of articles have followed Lowes' precedent. Nethercot did a good deal of source-hunting for "Christabel," but on a much more modest scale than that undertaken by Lowes. J. B. Beer in *Coleridge the Visionary* sought sources also, but he does more interpretation of the poems generally than Nethercot does of "Christabel." Critics are fascinated with tracing the numerous streams that proceed from Coleridge's deep wells of reading and reflection. But, unless the source-hunting leads to some interpretive insights, one wonders what the ultimate value of it is.

THE STUDY OF IMAGES

Another kind of detective work is image-hunting, looking for the use of figurative language in poems that can illuminate the whole poetic corpus. One of the most thorough and sensitive works in this area is Marshall Suther's recent book, *Visions of Xanadu*. He does not concern himself to any great extent with the approaches of historical criticism, but his demonstration of relationships between "Kubla Khan" and Coleridge's other poems is generally informative of many of the poet's abiding concerns. Professor Suther did some of this kind of study in his earlier book, *The Dark Night of Samuel Taylor Coleridge*, but the chief importance of this first book is probably in what it suggests of the nature of the "poetic experience," how that experience is related and not related to the actual writing of poetry. Mr. Suther's two books can help to illuminate some of the interrelationships between the religious and the poetic in Coleridge's thought and work. But, there is a tendency in these two books to ignore some important historical and biographical information that bears on the issues of Coleridge's religious faith and attitudes. Perhaps the point of view that Mr. Suther takes toward Coleridge stresses too much the mystical and ignores too much the Protestant. For a balance in one's study, a reading of Carl Woodring's *Politics in the Poetry of Coleridge* alongside Mr. Suther's books would be worthwhile.

A NEW EVALUATION OF OPIUM ADDICTION

There has been a drift in recent scholarship and criticism on Coleridge away from the opium business, that is, as a paramount concern in evaluating his work. Students of Coleridge seem presently to feel that the opium crisis in Coleridge's life has been too much emphasized in past times. After Elisabeth Schneider's scholarly work on the question, we have some substantial grounds for considering that Coleridge could have been a good poet and continued to be one whether he was an opium eater or not. But, this is not to say that everyone is now willing to consider his drug addiction an irrelevant factor in the evaluation of his career. We are probably ready to say that opium has been in the past too easy a way out of scholarly and critical difficulties.

COLERIDGE'S NOTEBOOKS

There has been in recent critical (and biographical) study more and more use made of Coleridge's notebooks, now available in the excellent scholarly edition of Miss Kathleen Coburn of Toronto. The Notebooks is part of the twenty-volume Collected Works of Coleridge, to be published in America by the Bollingen Foundation. When the whole of the Notebooks is completed, there will be an elaborate subject index to the greatly diverse materials included.

COLERIDGE'S LETTERS

Coleridge's letters, now gathered in a four-volume edition by Earl Leslie Griggs, published by Oxford, have continued to be an invaluable storehouse of information about the poet. The most obvious reason is that he wrote to one person or another nearly everything he ever thought or felt.

COLERIDGE AS LITERARY CRITIC

The books and articles that have been written on Coleridge as literary critic are more favorable than they are not. Irving Babbitt, F. L. Lucas, and F. R. Leavis have censored Coleridge for obscurity, and for claims to critical insight that could never be his. I. A. Richards and T. S. Eliot have been more generally impressed with Coleridge's criticism. I. A. Richards supports the distinction Coleridge made between Fancy and Imagination. Eliot has spoken of Coleridge as perhaps the greatest single critic of Shakespeare up to the present time. Cleanth Brooks has been impressed, as one might expect; with Coleridge's handling of paradox. John Crowe Ransom, expressing an attitude toward Coleridge that would probably be shared by all of the new critics, acclaims Coleridge as a great practitioner in criticism, pays tribute to his encyclopedic interests, but puts his foot down hard on Coleridge's meandering processes of thought and expression. Ransom considers Coleridge's critical language fantastic.

COLERIDGE AS THEOLOGIAN

Students of Coleridge as a theologian have been more generally favorable than students of his criticism-opinion, that is, has been more corporately complimentary of his work as a theologian. No one would deny the profound way he has changed the course of theological thought and action in England and America since his time. C. R. Sanders' book *Coleridge and the Broad Church Movement* is probably the most thorough study of Coleridge's theological influence to date, but this book is mainly about the later Coleridge. There has been no distinguished study of the theology of Coleridge's poetry to date. A critical study of the theological statements and implications in Coleridge's poems that penetrates deeply into his theological interests and connections during the time of his poetically fruitful years is much needed at present.

WILLIAM HAZLITT (1823)

"Coleridge had agreed to come over and see my father, according to the courtesy of the country, as Mr. Rowe's probable successor; but in the meantime, I had gone to hear him preach the Sunday after his arrival. A poet and a philosopher getting up into a Unitarian pulpit to preach the gospel, was a romance in these degenerate days, a sort of revival of the primitive spirit of Christianity, which was not to be resisted." "It was in January of 1798, that I rose one morning before daylight, to walk ten miles in the mud, to hear this celebrated person preach . . . When I got there, the organ was playing the 100th Psalm, and when it was done, Mr. Coleridge rose and gave out his text, 'And he went up into the mountain to pray, Himself, Alone.' As he gave out this text, his voice 'rose like a stream of rich distilled perfumes,' and when he came to the two last words, which he pronounced loud, deep, and distinct, it seemed to me, who was then young, as if the sounds had echoed from the bottom of the human heart, and as if that prayer might have floated in solemn silence through the universe. The idea of St. John came into my mind, 'of one crying in the wilderness, who had his loins girt about, and whose food was locusts and wild honey.' The preacher then launched into his subject, like an eagle dallying with the wind. The sermon was upon peace and war; upon church and state - not their alliance, but their separation - on the spirit of the world and the spirit of Christianity, not as the same, but as opposed to one another. He talked of those who had 'inscribed the cross of Christ on Banners dripping with human gore.' He made a poetical and pastoral excursion - and to shew the fatal effects of war, drew a striking contrast between the simple shepherd-boy, driving his team afield, or sitting under the hawthorn, piping to his flock, 'as though he should never be old,' and the same poor country-lad, crimped, kidnapped, brought into town, made drunk at an alehouse, turned into a wretched drummer-boy, with his hair sticking on end with powder and pomatum, a long cue at his back, and tricked out in the loathsome finery of the profession of blood . . . And for myself, I could not have been more delighted if I had heard the music of the spheres. Poetry and Philosophy had met together. Truth and Genius had embraced, under the eye and with the sanction of Religion. This was even beyond my hopes. I returned home well satisfied."

"Coleridge, in his person, was rather above the common size, inclining to the corpulent, or like Lord Hamlet, 'somewhat fat and pursy.' His hair (now, alas! grey) was then black and glossy as the raven's, and fell in smooth masses over his forehead. This long pendulous hair is peculiar to enthusiasts, to those whose minds tend heavenward; and is traditionally inseparable (though of a different color) from the pictures of Christ. It ought to belong, as a character, to all who preach Christ crucified, and Coleridge was at that time one of those!"

JOHN STUART MILL (1840)

"The time is yet far distant, when, in the estimation of Coleridge, and of his influence upon the intellect of our time, anything like unanimity can be looked for. As a poet, Coleridge has taken his place. The healthier taste, and more intelligent canons of poetic criticism, which he was himself mainly instrumental in diffusing, have at length assigned to him his proper rank, as one among the great (and, if we look to the powers shown rather than to the amount of actual achievement, among the greatest) names in our literature. But, as a philosopher, the class of thinkers has scarcely yet arisen by whom he is to be judged. The limited philosophical public of this country is as yet too exclusively divided between those to whom Coleridge and the views which he promulgated or defended are everything, and those to whom they are nothing."

MATTHEW ARNOLD (1863)

"Coleridge had less delicacy and penetration than Joubert, but more richness and power; his production, though far inferior to what his nature at first seemed to promise, was abundant and varied. Yet in all his production how much is there to dissatisfy us! How many reserves must be made in praising either his poetry, or his criticism, or his philosophy! How little either of his poetry, or of his criticism, or of his philosophy, can we expect permanently to stand! But that which will stand of Coleridge is this: the stimulus of his continual effort, - not a moral effort, for he had no morals, - but of his continual instinctive effort, crowned often with rich success, to get at and to lay bare the real truth of his matter in hand, whether that matter were literary, or philosophical, or political, or religious; and this in a country where at that moment such an effort was almost unknown; where the most powerful minds threw themselves upon poetry, which conveys truth, indeed, but conveys it indirectly; and where ordinary minds were so habituated to do without thinking altogether, to regard considerations of established routine and practical convenience as paramount, that any attempt to introduce within the domain of these the disturbing elements of thought, they were prompt to resent as an outrage. Coleridge's great usefulness lay in his supplying in England, for many years and under critical circumstances, by the spectacle of this effort of his, a stimulus to all minds capable of profiting by it, in the generation which grew up around him. His action will still be felt as long as the need for it continues. When, with the cessation of the need, the action too has ceased, Coleridge's memory, in spite of the disesteem - nay, repugnance - which his character may and must inspire, will yet for ever remain invested with that interest and gratitude which invests the memory of founders."

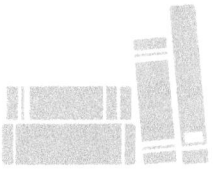

SAMUEL TAYLOR COLERIDGE

BIBLIOGRAPHY

EDITIONS OF COLERIDGE'S WORK

Brinkley, R.F., ed., *Coleridge on the Seventeenth Century* (Durham, North Carolina, 1955). Theological analyses of 17th-century theologians.

Campbell, James D., ed., *Poetical Works* (New York, 1893). Contains helpful biographical introduction and notes.

Coburn, Kathleen, ed., *Inquiring Spirit* (New York, 1951). Selections from Coleridge arranged by subject headings.

Coburn, Kathleen, ed., *The Notebooks of Samuel Taylor Coleridge*, 2 vols. (New York, 1957). A nearly inexhaustible mine of information about the poet's life and thought. Two volumes published by Bollingen Foundation so far. Miss Coburn's editorial notes often give insights into Coleridge's work unobtainable elsewhere.

Coburn, Kathleen, ed., *Philosophical Lectures of Samuel Taylor Coleridge* (London, 1949). The lectures of Coleridge given between 14 December and 29 March 1819. Informing introduction on Coleridge as a philosopher.

Coleridge, Ernest H., ed., *The Complete Poetical Works of Samuel Taylor Coleridge*, 2 vols. (London, 1962). The best edition of Coleridge's poetry and dramatic works. Contains variant readings.

Coleridge, Ernest H., ed., *The Poems of Samuel Taylor Coleridge* (London, 1961). Probably the most useful one-volume edition of the poetry. Does not contain the dramas.

Griggs, Earl L., ed., *Collected Letters of Samuel Taylor Coleridge*, 4 vols. (Oxford, 1956). The most complete edition of the letters to date. Contains many illuminating editorial comments.

Raysor, Thomas M., ed., *Shakespearean Criticism*, 28 vols. (London, 1960). Corrects the editorial work of H. N. Coleridge, gives the shorthand notes on the lectures taken by two persons who attended the lectures. Valuable introduction and notes.

Shawcross, John, ed., *Biographia Literaria*, 2 vols. (London, 1962). Contains valuable introduction and notes to Coleridge's famous and infamous critical work.

Shedd, William G. T., ed., The *Complete Works of Samuel Taylor Coleridge*, 7 vols. (New York, 1860). To date this is one of the nearest approaches to a complete edition of Coleridge's works. The other is Thomas Ashe, 8 vols. (Bohn's Library), 1865, 1884 - 1885. Both will be superceded by the Bollingen Foundation edition when it is completed.

BIOGRAPHY

Armour, Richard W. and Raymond F. Howes, eds., *Coleridge the Talker: A Series of Contemporary Descriptions and Comments* (Ithaca, 1940). Contemporary accounts of Coleridge's conversations. Coleridge the talker is the essential Coleridge; the other sides of the man are subsidiary.

Campbell, J. D., *Samuel Taylor Coleridge; a Narrative of the Events of his Life* (London, 1894). At one time the standard life of Coleridge. Now replaced by Hanson and Chambers.

Carlyon, Clement, *Early Years and Late Reflections*, 4 vols. (London, 1836 - 58). Recollections of Coleridge's stay in Germany. Coleridge's impact on people in Göttingen.

Chambers, E. K., *Samuel Taylor Coleridge* (Oxford, 1938). Covering the whole life, but, of course, not containing the detail of Hanson on the early years. Helpful chronology but too censorious in places to be accurate.

Flagg, J. B., ed., *The Life and Letters of Washington Allston* (New York, 1892). Allston and Coleridge formed a strong friendship during Coleridge's years in Malta.

Gillman, James, *Life of Samuel Taylor Coleridge* (London, 1838). Biography by the man who gave Coleridge a home for the last eighteen years of his life.

Hanson, Lawrence, *The Life of Samuel Taylor Coleridge: The Early Years* (New York, 1962). This biography covers Coleridge's life only to June, 1800, but for those years it is the best available source. Full and useful notes.

Knight, W. A., *Coleridge and Wordsworth in the West Country: Their Friendship, Work and Surroundings* (New York, 1914). A collection of letters and diaries, extracts from Dorothy Wordsworth's Journal for the years 1795 - 98.

Margoliouth, H. M., *Wordsworth and Coleridge*, 1795 - 1834 (New York, 1953). Valuable for the study of interrelationships.

Potter, Stephen, *Coleridge and S. T. C.* (London, 1935). A study of the stronger and weaker sides of Coleridge's personality. The true Coleridge was the artist.

Potter, Stephen, ed., *Minnow Among Tritons; Mrs. S. T. Coleridge's letters to Thomas Poole*, 1799 - 1834 (London, 1934). In Mrs. Coleridge's letters to her husband's dear friend, many interesting facets of the poet's life emerge.

Watson, Lucy E. G., *Coleridge at Highgate* (New York, 1925). The poet's life is surveyed from 1816 until his death. The author is the granddaughter of Dr. Gillman. Very sympathetic with Coleridge.

Whalley, George, *Coleridge and Sara Hutchinson and the Asra Poems* (London, 1955). A study of Coleridge's relationship with Sara Hutchinson and the poetic results of it. Very interesting for its study of Sara Hutchinson.

CRITICISM

Baker, James V., *The Sacred River, Coleridge's Theory of the Imagination* (New Orleans, 1957). Almost entirely on Coleridge's criticism, but there is some attention to poems. Cf. "Coleridge's writings cited" in the "Subject Index."

Beer, J. B., *Coleridge the Visionary* (New York, 1962). Valuable critical work in that it balances the search for sources and the concern to trace recurrent archetypal myths with illuminating interpretive criticism. Some reference to historical matters.

Beyer, Werner W., *The Enchanted Forest* (New York, 1963). More source hunting in the direction of the influences of Wieland's *Oberon* on Coleridge. Profitable interpretive work also.

Bodkin, Maud, *Archetypal Patterns in Poetry* (London, 1934). Readings of "The Ancient Mariner" and "Kubla Khan" within the categories of Jung's archetypes.

Bostetter, Edward E., *The Romantic Ventriloquists* (Seattle, 1963). A compact and penetrating essay on Coleridge is included in this study of the major English Romantics. Bostetter's approach tends toward the existentialist.

Boulger, James D., *Coleridge as Religious Thinker* (New Haven, 1961). Mr. Boulger does not concern himself with Coleridge's poetry, although he does have a final chapter on "Religion and Poetry." As the title states, the book is particularly concerned with the later Coleridge, the theologian.

House, Humphry, *Coleridge* (London, 1953). Highly praised essays on Coleridge's poetic attitudes and major poems. Included are "The Eolian Harp," "Frost at Midnight," "The Ancient Mariner," "Kubla Khan," "Christabel," and "Dejection: An Ode."

Knight, G. Wilson, *The Starlit Dome* (London, 1941). Highly suggestive readings, but Mr. Knight's interpretations should not be the only ones the student reads.

Lowes, John Livingston, *The Road to Xanadu* (Boston, 1964). The great detective work in Coleridge criticism. Professor Lowes sought to find the sources for all Coleridge's images in "The Rime of the Ancient Mariner" and in "Kubla Khan." The work moves much beyond this ambition, however, in its ". . . Study in the Ways of the Imagination."

Suther, Marshall, *The Dark Night of Samuel Taylor Coleridge.* (New York, 1960). A study of Coleridge as a mystic who failed as a poet because he sought both in poetry and in love a mystical experience of the Absolute. An interesting point of view on Coleridge, but it needs the correction of certain angles of historical criticism.

Suther, Marshall, *Visions of Xanadu* (New York, 1965). The second of Professor Suther's books on Coleridge is a book-length study of "Kubla Khan" in relationship to the whole corpus of his poetry. Again more the psychological, religious approach than the historical.

Warren, Robert Penn, "A Poem of Pure Imagination," in edition of "The Rime of the Ancient Mariner" (New York, 1946). One of the most famous essays written on the poem to date.

Woodring, Carl R., *Politics in the Poetry of Coleridge* (Madison, 1961). An absolutely indispensable book for students of Coleridge's poetry. A wealth of scholarship. Persons who think that clarity and eloquence reside only in the use of polysyllabic words should study Mr. Woodring's style.

www.ingramcontent.com/pod-product-compliance
Ingram Content Group UK Ltd.
Pitfield, Milton Keynes, MK11 3LW, UK
UKHW020719050526
12271UKWH00018B/228